THE SUM OF HER PARTS

THE SUM OF HER PARTS

Essays

SIÂN GRIFFITHS

The University of Georgia Press   *Athens*

Published by the University of Georgia Press
Athens, Georgia 30602
www.ugapress.org
© 2022 by Siân Griffiths
All rights reserved
Designed by Erin Kirk
Set in Arno Pro
Printed and bound by Sheridan Books
The paper in this book meets the guidelines for
permanence and durability of the Committee on
Production Guidelines for Book Longevity of the
Council on Library Resources.

Most University of Georgia Press titles are
available from popular e-book vendors.

Printed in the United States of America
26   25   24   23   22   P   5   4   3   2   1

Library of Congress Control Number: 2022930664
ISBN: 9780820362335 (paperback)
ISBN: 9780820362342 (ebook)

For my mother

and for my mothers

For my sister

and for my sisters

Contents

THE SUM OF HER PARTS

Parts

X = component of a thing
X + y = a celebration
    = a group waiting for seats at a table
X + ner = half of a team (as in business, romance, tennis)
playing a X = inhabiting a role
X + ial = not the whole
        = biased
        = attracted (to)
Xs is Xs = slogan implicating inferior nuggets
doing my X = doing what's expected
just doing my X = doing far more than expected
X + ido = game, *Spanish*
X + ing = sweet sorrow
de + X = leave
de + X + ed = dead, gone
dear(ly) de + X + ed = never gone
X = the skull's dividing line, as hair defines its hemispheres
im + X = to deliver (wisdom)
+   im + X + ial = without opinions or bias, an inhuman state

a whole, or something greater?

Cunt

The guy calls on a Monday, leaving a message on the office voicemail, but it is his minutes-later follow-up email I receive first. He introduces himself as a graduate student thinking about taking my summer fiction writing class. The only problem? He thinks my absence policy is too strict. He "has questions" about it.

My policy outlines the penalty students will incur on their participation scores if they miss class, suggesting that they drop the course if they are going to miss excessive sessions. It's a policy I've arrived at after fifteen years of teaching college-level classes, a policy that makes it clear that students must be in class. I expect them to take their education as seriously as I do.

He calls it "inhuman" in his phone message, repeating that word when he flags me down after my night class. As we talk, he tells me that he had another professor with a strict absence policy when he was an undergrad. He missed a week for medical reasons, and it devastated his course grade. "She failed me," he says, "and I was, like, 'Well, you're a cunt.'"

Cunt. The word lashes out.

No, that's not accurate. That's only how I feel it. From his stance, it is more casual. Something to be slung around, dropped, forgotten.

To clarify, I know that he isn't calling *me* a cunt, though I have the potential to be one. I understand, too, that he did not use this word directly to this nameless professor. He is talking about his feelings, representing them in words. This is his gut-level thought response. Still, I am speechless.

Speechless and already questioning my own reaction. The kid seems well spoken and intelligent. And not only well spoken but soft spoken. His mouth wraps the word "cunt" in bunny fur. He laughs and smiles, almost but not quite blushing, his face boyish and jovial. "You have to ignore curse words from me," he says. "They're just part of who I am." Later he adds, "I'm queer. We use that word in my community."

I have so many feelings. I comb through them.

The one I'm surest of is this: The context in which he has used the word is hateful. He is not reclaiming a word made ugly by anger. He applies "cunt" disparagingly to a female professor, throwing her gender at her like a grenade. And in this, his first-ever interaction with me, he includes me in that grenade's collateral damage.

I think, too, that he has a clear misunderstanding of how words work if he believes that he can single-handedly define their meaning, as if they hold no communally determined denotations or connotations. As if they have no history.

He's also ignoring our current context. We are not two drag queens trading banter. I am a professor, not a friend. In social terms, I am closer to the woman he described than I am to him. This is a professional interaction. I am a person who, if he takes my course, will grade his work and write letters of reference and support his career—or not.

Finally, he ignores what is likely to be my own personal context. Hugh Rawson's *Dictionary of Invective* calls *cunt* "the most heavily tabooed of all English words." The *Oxford English Dictionary* agrees, saying, "In spite of its widespread use over a long period and in many sections of society, there remains a strong taboo concerning use of this word." It adds that "its public use has often been prohibited or restricted, notably in news and broadcast media" and "Until relatively recently it appeared only rarely in print." Even without such sources, this student can assume that I have seen and heard the word used to deride women. That's what context does: it creates a set of shared assumptions by which we can navigate our word choices. Yes, I've also heard *cunt* used playfully, and I know how to recognize the difference, but that is something less safe to assume, and his tone was not playful.

Even as I sort through all these arguments, knowing I could articulate at least some of them, they go unspoken because (1) it is 8:30 at night, I've been on campus for twelve hours, and I want to go home, and (2) I don't want to look like a prude.

Prude: a word invoked to goad women into performing actions they find shameful and, further, to prevent them from speaking out against ideas and behaviors they find offensive. *Prude*: an electric cattle prod of a word, a word designed to put us into the old binaries of virgin/whore, good/evil, nerd/cool, Sandra Dee/Rizzo, naïveté/knowledge.

And what do I do with his announcement that he is queer, or the assumption that this should allow him to use *cunt* casually? Throughout my career, I have prevented straight students from silencing the stories of their gay and lesbian classmates. Some students have called LGBTQ-themed work "inappropriate for class," but I insist otherwise. More than once, students have refused to read their peers' work, as if refusal to read were a moral stance, but writers do not have the right to determine each other's subject matter. Just as my conservative students have the right to express their political and religious beliefs, so my LGBTQ students should write toward their convictions, giving voice to experiences others would prefer closeted and unspoken. Defending free speech is fundamental to my beliefs.

If I silence this student's word choice, am I infringing on his rights or merely defending my own? No, this is not a story written for class. It's his life story, related here in a campus hallway. The distinction is, in many ways, academic.

His words are laced with a subtext that I don't want to acknowledge. Even as I try to unhear it, I'm aware that his speech is underwritten by the assumption that his status as a gay man supersedes my status as a woman. His context is more important than my context. His announcement that "it's OK because I'm queer" implies that, rather than ignoring my reasons for balking at the word, he dismisses them outright.

I don't like my own awareness of his words' implications. Can he really be suggesting that gay men have a greater claim to power and privilege? Does he believe that, straight or gay, men have a greater right to set the terms of the conversation (let alone class policies) than women?

I don't want us split, staring each other down from opposite sides of a dichotomy. We should be fighting together in an ongoing battle against larger oppressive social forces. Thinking even for a moment that his words position us against one another feels gross and uncomfortable. I don't want to have to figure out our relative positions on the great chain of being, the invisible hierarchy of oppressions determining so much of our daily lives. I'm sick of hierarchy. I'm sick of being aware of it.

Then again, he's speaking off the cuff, not thinking his words out or editing. I too say things that imply beliefs I don't have—we all do. We're sloppy with the spoken word.

Other students, male and female, have told me that I should be home raising my children, that my children must be confused about who their mother is and whether I love them. These comments have come openly. On the scale of insulting comments, calling another professor a cunt isn't the worst I've heard. I want to forgive him his gaffe.

Perhaps, I think hopefully, he sees using the word as a way of including me in his group, a person with whom he can throw "cunt" around. I would defend a community's right to take a word back, to reclaim. I'd love to think he's including me.

Yet I hear that assumption of superiority in his word choice, and I see him ignore the fact that his usage isn't reclaiming the word at all. He is using it in exactly the hateful spirit in which "cunt" evolved to be an invective. His phrasing suggests that she slighted him not because of legitimate educational concerns but because she has a vagina and is therefore mean spirited and shrewish or worse.

He's claiming another privilege—a privilege I have defended for so many students, gay and straight, if not for him in particular. He wants not only the power to speak but to use language on his own terms and determine its meaning. I want him and writers everywhere to feel some ownership with language. It allows them to play, to nudge words a little here and there, to make us see words fresh and understand them in new and profound ways.

Only, he's forgotten that language is always a negotiation between user and receiver, between text and subtext, text and context. He has forgotten that, ultimately, we get just a little room to play because words are embedded in weighty histories. He has forgotten that every speaker requires a listener. He is a tree falling in the woods, but I am there to hear him. To be crushed.

Should I tell him this? Should I start the argument? Will I look like exactly the malicious, inhuman woman he assumes me to be? Will he think I'm close minded or, worse, homophobic? My mind floods with questions like too much gas in an engine. I find myself again and again unstarting. Has the moment to speak passed? What reaction is he hoping for? That I will be so invested in not wanting to be thought of as a cunt that I will drop the knowledge of experience and change my policies to appease him? Does he think I'm so desperate for him to enroll?

Underneath these questions is the rumble of one thundering thought: How *dare* he use a vagina as a tool against me!

Then again, he's just a twenty-something-year-old kid.

A kid who sees me as inhuman. Or, at least, a kid who sees my syllabus as inhuman. But my syllabus is also an extension of me, the version of the professor me that I commit to the page in the form of policies and readings and assignments and schedules. He lobbed that word at me twice, I remind myself, before he stabbed with the sharper-bladed word. He, a consumer of education, is unhappy. I, the automaton professor, am to blame. He is the only human here. As the customer, he feels sure he is right.

I don't silence the student. I don't explain. I allow his words to silence me. Or, I allow my exhaustion to silence me. It's late and growing later. I haven't seen my children since getting them out of bed this morning. I don't want to be the harpy. I want to be cool, open minded, fun. I don't want to get into it. All I want is to ask my kids about their day, put them to bed, make a sandwich, and sit in a quiet room where no one wants anything from me.

"If he enrolls," I tell myself, "we'll deal with this then."

A colleague tells me that this is how to recognize microaggression: the exhaustion of not wanting to explain what you've already explained in a million other contexts, a million other times. I wonder about this. Confronting a professor three times (by phone, by email, in person) about her absence policy—a policy and syllabus that was already vetted and approved by the Master of Arts Steering Committee—doesn't feel like microaggression or passive aggression. It's open aggression. It says: I, a man, have decided to bring you, a woman, into line. It says: I reject your role as a professor. It says: I know better than you.

For two days I parse the situation. I decide I'm not going to pursue it, and then I am, and then I'm not. It's a slip, but it suggests a lack of boundaries and respect. I don't want to be guided by a bruised ego. I want to make certain I am not being vindictive. I decide to ask our graduate coordinator if anyone has had problems with this student.

"No," she says, then pauses, turning to face me fully. "Are you?"

I sink into a chair. "I'm not sure." I tell her about the phone call, the email, the hallway conversation. I confess I'm at a loss for what to do and that I'm fairly certain the answer is "nothing." I missed my chance. Finally I ask if he has earned one of the teaching assistantships reserved for our strongest students.

Yes, it turns out. The Masters Committee awarded him an assistantship the previous morning. He will teach Freshman Composition this fall.

I do not think of my vagina as a cunt. I do not think of it as a pussy or a box or a tuna boat or a honey pot or a snatch or a vertical smile or a bearded clam or sugar walls or a muff or a cock socket or a coochie or anything fishy. To be honest, I do not even think of it as a vagina. Unless I must name it, I don't. I disavow the history of malice entwined in "cunt," and I cringe at the cold anatomical sound of "vagina." These names, all names, were constructed by others. I don't want to reclaim any of them. I'm uninterested.

It is a part of me, a defining characteristic that I keep to myself and yet wear on every inch of my skin. It maps the layout of my bones. It is my greatest vulnerability, the place where I am penetrable. I want to call it my strength as well, but that may be going too far. What it provides is akin to strength but separate from the masculine ideal that "strength" normally evokes. I have no idea to what extent it defines my personality or limits my options. I can imagine, have imagined, the amputation of various body parts, the loss of a finger, the plucking of an eye, the severed foot. My vagina is part of my core, unsegmentable from the whole.

I know that this guy had no thought of my vagina when he threw "cunt" at me. To him it was just a word, something he could attach to his sentence's vocabulary as he chose.

But a feminine word, slanderous and condemning.

I am reading etymologies this morning, curious about how my parts were named. I know enough about four-letter words to know that they tend to be our oldest bits of language. Fuck, shit, cock, cunt: you don't replace a word that visceral, that handy.

At the risk of sounding like Hermione Granger, I will say that if you ever want some entertaining reading, the online *Oxford English Dictionary*'s litany of historical usages is pretty great. I can't resist sharing a sample:

> 1638 in J. Addy *Sin & Society in 17th Cent.* (1989) ix. 128 A cuntsomoner of the bawdy court.

> c1650 in J. W. Hales & F. J. Furnivall *Bp. Percy's Folio MS: Loose & Humorous Songs* (1867) 99 Vp start the Crabfish, & catcht her by the Cunt.

> 1680 Earl of Rochester et al. *Poems* 28 Her Hand, her Foot, her very look's a Cunt.

> 1865 'Philocomus' *Love Feast* iii. 21, I faint! I die! I spend! My cunt is sick! Suck me and fuck me!

> c1890 *My Secret Life* VII. 161, I sicken with desire, pine for unseen, unknown cunts.

I'm tickled by the breadth and creativity of the references as well as by their frankness. They play off the monosyllable slap of the word. How can a foot or a hand be also a cunt? What does it mean to be a cuntsomoner? Why, in the 1800s, does the word become paired with sickness? How strange, to find male desire portrayed not as potency or virility but weakness.

Here in the *OED*, the word loses the power to offend. I am merely fascinated, merely a childishly delighted scholar. I feel like a sixth grader again, giggling over the dirty words in our classroom Webster: fart, vagina, penis, poop. Huddled in our intimate circle, my classmates and I knew we were on treacherous ground. We kept a lookout for our teacher, ready to point to some innocent word on the page. We had learned that research should be restricted to the chaste and the boring, a terrible lesson I wouldn't unlearn until graduate school.

I'm again aware of the split in me. The writer-scholar part of me thrills with the love of language, the curiosity, the feeling that education should be boundless and borderless and anything but prudish.

The first listing for cunt is this:

> c1230 in M. Gelling & D. M. Stenton *Place-names Oxfordshire* (1953) I. 40 (*MED*), Gropecuntelane.

A street name. The *OED*'s etymology notes: "The word is recorded earliest in place names, bynames, and surnames," adding that "some twenty instances of this name are recorded throughout the country, at least six of them in the 13th cent., although all are now lost."

"It has . . . been suggested," the *OED* continues, "that the word was applied at an early date to certain topographical features, such as a cleft in a small hill or mound (in e.g. *Cuntelowe*, Warwickshire (1221; now lost)), a wooded gulley or valley (in e.g. *Kuntecliue*, Lancashire (1246, now Lower Cunliffe), *Cuntewellewang*, Lincolnshire (1317; now lost)), and a cleft with a stream running through it (in e.g. *Cuntebecsic* (field name), Caistor, Lincolnshire (a1272; now lost), *Shauecuntewelle*, Kent (1321; earlier as *Savetuntewell* (1275), now Shinglewell))." I am delighted. What a metaphor! To think that a cunt was not always something hidden, but just another body part that might name a location, mundane as a finger or leg. It names such pretty landscapes.

The erasure of the cunt from place-names is somehow slightly Edenic, as if those ancient Britons suddenly became aware of sin and felt the need to cover that nakedness. Its removal suggests a change in mindset about sexuality in general and female sexuality in particular. The word acquired the tint of shame.

By the third entry, we are into anatomy books.

a1400 tr. Lanfranc *Sci. Cirurgie* (Ashm.) (1894) 172 In wymmen þe necke of þe bladdre is schort, & is maad fast to the cunte.

It is one of a handful of medical references among the samples, confirming that the word was not always vulgar. The word continues to appear even after the introduction of Latin anatomical terms, including *vagina* (meaning "sheath, scabbard," though this anatomical sheath would house a different kind of sword altogether), in the late 1600s. In addition to the 1400 entry, I find

a1425 *Medulla Gram.* (Stonyhurst) f. 70ᵛ, *Vulua*, a count or a wombe.

Also, it lists this much later medical advice:

1743 H. Walpole *Little Peggy* in *Corr.* (1961) XXX. 309 Distended cunts with alum shall be braced.

How does a word, once so mundane, become recognized by the *OED* in 2014 as "the strongest swear word in English"?

I look up *Sin and Society* to find the context for Addy's "cuntsomoner" and find more verbal play. The passage deals with church courts, which Addy notes were more concerned with "scandalous living" than with heresy. The court was popularly called the "bawdy court," and the apparitor or court summoner became the "cuntsomoner." Addy notes that "such comments the court officials could not allow to pass uncorrected since they could lead to the authority of the court being ignored with impunity." Thus play mingled with slight, and insult threatened injury. Here in 1638, "cunt" has become a word to aim at someone. The word straddles bawdy hijinks and mean-spirited slur.

We witness the word inhabiting both these spaces in the other examples from the time. In the 1650s *Loose and Humorous Songs*, a husband places a crab he has purchased in a chamber pot, and as his wife stoops to pee, she is caught in that most delicate of places. I've updated the spelling for easier reading, but the raunchy comedy propelling the poem is timeless:

Alas," quoth the goodwife, "that ever I was born,
the devil is in the piss pot, and has me on his horn."

Her husband's misguided attempt to free her by blowing on the crab (!) results in the crab pinching him on the nose, and thus the two are left until, responding to the husband's call "with great wonder," the neighbors come to the rescue "to part his wife's tail & his nose asunder." Here the cunt is something slightly illicit, but the shame is still able to evoke humor.

In 1680 the Earl of Rochester uses "cunt" throughout his poetry collection in scenes of romantic love, in some of the most explicit descriptions I've seen in seventeenth-century poetry:

> In liquid raptures I dissolve all o'er,
> Melt into sperm, and spend every pore.
> A touch from any part of her had done 't:
> Her hand, her foot, her very look's a cunt.

The word here merely names the female body with the same openness that he names his own. Yet in that same collection he uses "cunt" more dismissively, applying it to Mrs. Sue Willis, a prostitute operating "on the fringes of the court circle," according to the gloss:

> Bawdy in thoughts, precise in words,
>   Ill-natured though a whore,
> Her belly is a bag of turds,
>   And her cunt a common shore.

The OED lists Samuel Pepys's Diary (1663) as the first use of "cunt" to mean "prostitute,"[1] but in this earlier poem we can already see the word evolving in that direction. The Earl of Rochester asks us to judge this woman harshly. Here the cunt is compared to landscape as in medieval geographical names, but the metaphor is reversed, the vagina like a shore rather than a shore like a vagina, and this reversal is damning.

---

1 "Sir Charles Sydly . . . showed his nakedness—acting all the postures of lust and buggery that could be imagined, and . . . saying that there he hath to sell such a pouder as should make all the cunts in town run after him."

The *OED* lists definitions in the order each new usage can be found in written text, so we can see how the word evolves one meaning from its previous meanings. Perusing the list of definitions for "cunt," I witness the word's evolution, from a reference to female genitalia, to the woman—the slut—herself, to the act of having sexual intercourse, to an abusive term for a man, to any despised, unpleasant, or annoying thing.

There it is: *Slut. Abusive. Despised.* Desire commingles with the despicable. By 1755 "cunt" was too foul to be included in Samuel Johnson's dictionary, nor would it appear in any major dictionary of English for two more centuries, first appearing in the United States in the 1961 *Webster's Third New International Dictionary* and in Great Britain in the 1965 *Penguin English Dictionary*. When James Joyce wrote "the grey sunken cunt of the world" in *Ulysses*, what other word could be as harsh?

The graduate coordinator relays my story to the Master of Arts, English Program director, and he comes to my office. He wants the story again. Already I'm sick of telling it, but I do, telling it honestly, aiming to be fair. Just the facts, ma'am.

He asks the question I've known is coming ever since he told me he wanted to talk. "What do you think we should do?"

The tiredness sets in again, a bone-deep kind of gravitational pull. I don't want to suggest punishments or steps to be taken. I don't want to be responsible for what happens to a student who isn't even *my* student. This seems to be the director's decision, the one he's best suited to make, since he was not involved in the incident. At the same time, I don't want female students, whether his peers or those he'll teach, to get caught in this same fugue.

I tell the director that, for my own part, I don't care. I tell him it's water under the bridge. I tell him my only concern is for the other students in the class who might also be subjected to his language and biases. I tell him the word was only a small part of the problem, the badgering over policies and his lack of respect another. I tell him that if this student enrolls in my class, he and I can revisit our discussion.

"I'll talk to him," the director says. "I'll let you know how it goes."

"You don't have to tell me," I insist. "I don't need to know."

I want to be done with this. I feel certain I know what the student will say: he didn't know any better, didn't mean to offend. He'll say again that his language is just part of who he is. He'll say maybe I shouldn't be so easily offended. He'll say all the things that suggest that I am, in fact, the problem.

Like any word, "cunt" has seen an ebb and flow in its usage, a lull from the Victorian era through the chaste 1950s leading to a recent resurgence. If we look at the frequency of its use in written texts since 1600, when the word "vagina" begins to replace it in medical texts, the graph is startling (see chart generated using Google Books Ngram Viewer). While still relatively rare in print, the appearance of this once tabooed invective is growing sharply.

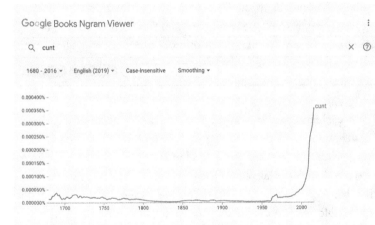

What the graph doesn't show is context, and so I am left to speculate. I know from my dictionary research that the early spike in the graph largely reflects an anatomical usage, though Samuel Pepys and others had also employed it to denote prostitutes by this point. I might further speculate that it was precisely *because* the word was sullied by this new definition that "vagina" was introduced. A replacement word was necessary for those with more delicate sensibilities. I'm assuming a causality that might not be accurate—perhaps it was the other way, the clinical, academic new word creating its binary, a vulgarity. Regardless of which word was chicken and which egg, by the nineteenth century "cunt" had nearly disappeared from written usage.

In the present day, "cunt" predominantly appears in insults, whether those insults be thrown around in jest or in earnest. That upward momentum looks almost unstoppable.

I am an ardent lover of language, in no small part because of its ability to morph. One of the reasons I love teaching is that my students, hip to the latest slang, keep me abreast of some of these changes. While I was drafting this essay, they began using "friendzone" as a verb ("OMG—she just friendzoned him!"). "Daydrinking" began popping up in tweets like pansies through snow, unexpected but beautiful. Words fall in and out of fashion; their popularity swells and subsides. We rarely stop to question the cause or effect of these trends. William S. Burroughs said, "Language is a virus," but now words go viral and somehow what's viral has lost the connotation of sickness.

Perhaps cunt's tide is surging. Perhaps this student is merely surfing that wave.

Yet context, context. I suspect that rise is part of something deeper, broader, more nefarious. Just as a new wave of racism swelled in recent years, gender tensions are rising. At a local Utah high school, girls discovered that their yearbook photos had been altered, "shirts" airbrushed onto their bare shoulders because we have so fetishized the female body that bare shoulders are obscene. The television haunts me with portrayals of the rape of Sansa Stark, and I can't determine if viewers are supposed to be disturbed, aroused, or some complex combination of those feelings. Salary inequity persists. Movie theaters show Captain America and Iron Man and the Hulk, with their female counterparts inhabiting supporting roles.[2] Social media fill with pictures of a Stanford swimmer given a mere

2 Black Widow's backstory tells that she would have preferred to be a mother but had been sterilized against her will. The Scarlet Witch falls into a weeping emotional mess in major battles.

six-month sentence for rape. The news reports Donald Trump's hateful invectives against Hillary Clinton and female reporters, but so many of my Bernie Bro friends are no more forgiving. They call her shrill, manipulative, and deceitful. They talk as if describing Eve herself, as if a woman in power precipitates a fall.

I stare at cunt's graph. The surge is massive. I cannot locate the moon that is pulling this tide. Is there one or many? How much hate is in the world? How much misogyny? I don't know how to fight such incredible gravity.

I wonder what I would name my parts.

At first I wrote, "Given the opportunity, I wonder what I would name my parts," but I have that opportunity. I resist it. Trying to determine why, I only arrive at this: I don't want to part and parcel myself.

Where does a cunt end and the rest of a woman's body begin? The evolution of the word suggests no separation, the cunt eclipsing the woman, the part becoming the whole. Something about that feels true, even as I reject the word as a descriptor. I am not a body part, and yet that part cannot be separated. My part, the hormones related to gender, the experiences that have formed me over time. These constitute who I am on a biological and psychological level. Laid on a table like the formaldehyde-soaked worms in science class, there's no point to place the scalpel. Naming the part feels similar; it's a segmenting off, a vivisection.

If I could turn back the clock on "cunt," restoring the word to anatomy, again a syllable innocent enough to be merely landscape, I think I might like the word.

This thought is irrelevant. I can't wish away history. I can't erase time or the communities of people who have agreed that a woman's vagina equates to the most insulting vulgarity in our language. "Cunt" has been too ravaged. It is a fallen word.

Still, I half love the ballsy bluntness of medieval language. I'm no specialist on the period, but sometimes it seems like those inhabitants of the Middle Ages were more progressive than we give them credit for—

especially in their attitudes toward women and sexuality. I remember the woman who locked a man in her tower until he agreed to marry her, or Margery Kempe ignoring her husband's desires so that she might pursue her own visions, strange as they were, and author her own book, perhaps the first autobiography in the English language. Those women had so much agency. Sure, the jokes of the time were lewd, but that frank sexuality also allowed women to be open with their desires, both in and outside the bedroom.

Study history long enough, and it makes you question the idea of progress.

I don't hear from the graduate director. I don't know what comes of the interview with the offending student. Probably nothing. Which is fine. I begin the summer session with an incredible class of graduate students, each smart and questioning and alight with curiosity and creativity and humor. I am content in my body, in my intellect, and in my curiosity.

Sir Kenneth Robinson once accused academics as seeing their bodies as nothing more than a form of transport for their minds, "a way of getting their heads to meetings." My major professor used to refer reverentially to "the life of the mind." I resist the romance of the intellect. My body is important to me. I am happier on a tennis court or on a horse or on a dance floor than in the classroom. Yet I, too, have been guilty of living in my head. Also, I know this, my head is biology, is body. Funny how the female brain, though physiologically different from the male brain, has no distinct word. No one names me by that part. In language, my brain cannot supersede my whole. Experience has suggested the opposite.

Here I am: a body and a mind, a cunt-centered thing and a series of thoughts about cunt-centered things.

Weeks into the summer semester, I walk into class to find my female students talking about the offending student, trading stories from their other classes where he dominates the conversation. They complain that he talks over them, not allowing them to finish their points. My scrupulously polite African student relates how he once covered the table they shared with his books. When she asked him to make space for her computer, he refused. Another student tells about a time he arrived late to class and asked her to move seats because she was in the chair he wanted. A third complains about him getting up noisily in the middle of her presentation. "Though, to be fair," she adds, "it was the end of the class time, and he had a bus to catch." The student next to her shakes her head. "He didn't have to be so *loud*."

I listen aghast. These offenses, one after another after another, happened in view of their professors, but none were commented on, none reprimanded, none even deemed worthy of notice. "Did you say anything to the guy?" I asked, pretending that I don't know the student they discussed.

"No," they say. They say he intimidates them, even though he may not mean to. He's big and strong and they don't know what he would do. Probably nothing, but still.

They can tell I am outraged on their behalf. "It's OK," they tell me. "It's really no big deal."

And perhaps it isn't. Haven't I seen the same kinds of actions from hundreds of other guys, well-meaning and otherwise, over the course of my own education? This shouldn't feel different. But it does.

My students know I don't usually back down from fights. They don't know that, in my one and only conversation with this guy, I did exactly that: I flinched.

"You should feel safer than that," I tell them. "We, your professors, should be looking out for you." I mean myself in particular. I wonder how much I would have seen if I were teaching that class. Would I have noticed if the students didn't call attention to the guy's behavior? Would I have heard the quiet request for desk space or commented on him speaking over his female peers? Sometimes, the space between the front of the classroom and the desks themselves feels capacious. I remind myself to watch with keener eyes.

If I believed that this one man was the problem, it would be easier to solve, but he is a symptom of an epidemic. Male domination of class discussion is widely documented. "Manspreading" has become a word that needs no definition for women who've repeatedly pinched themselves inward, ceded shared armrests, or pushed their chairs closer to the wall. "Mansplaining" appeared in similar fashion. Naming the concept allows us to perceive it, just as looking at the surging popularity of "cunt" allows me to perceive a broad-spread hate.

I believe in the power of words. I believe language shapes thought and experience, creates beauty and ugliness, and allows understanding and misunderstanding. Words reflect our fundamental beliefs, diminishing or amplifying those beliefs according to the diction that frames them. Words can assault. They can heal. Nothing about this feels petty or small.

That night, the student had only the expression on my face to read, which was inarticulate. His response was to entrench rather than to apologize. I talked only of absences and policy, avoiding the larger issues of language and authority and respect, avoiding the issue of gender altogether. I convinced myself it was an isolated slip.

This essay is my make-up call.

This essay is my wake-up call.

It is not enough for me to bear witness to language. Hate is malignant, but I am not without tools. I need to enter long conversations, even at night when I am tired and want to go home and feed my body and hug my kids. I want a better world for them, one that doesn't dismiss them based on gender or sexuality. I want to change the pendulum's swing. Silence is not an option. I can no longer be tired.

POSTSCRIPT

In July 2020 on a Saturday morning that seemed less like weekend and more like any other workday of the Covid lockdown, I opened an email no university professor wants to receive. It was from my university's Affirmative Action/Equal Opportunity officer asking me to call him as soon as possible. Baffled, I dialed.

He asked if I remembered the student in this essay, and I said I did, now even more at a loss. I'd written my essay during Trump's campaign for the presidency, and now we were in its last year, though we did not yet know it. The student had graduated and we had both moved on—or so I thought.

I learned that the student had read my essay and called to complain. In fact, the AA/EO officer was the last in a long string of administrators whom he had contacted. The student argued that I had committed libel in writing this piece, though he did not refute any of the facts. Mostly he was upset that I had implied that he was a misogynist. Though I had not named him, he felt that he could be identified, and he did not want my essay to cost him future employment.

The call was amicable enough. Our AA/EO officer told me that he had read my essay, as had my department chair, as had my dean, as had the university's legal team. The lawyers saw no grounds for a lawsuit, and after some pleasant chat, the AA/EO officer concluded the call by saying that his office would not be taking any action. He had promised the student that he would relay the pain I had caused, and asked me to be careful if I wrote about students in the future. I said that I would.

I did not say that I planned for this essay to lead off the collection that I had been drafting. Here I have eliminated some physical description, though I doubted whether the essay would harm him even if he were identified. In my own department, where this student's offenses were witnessed and reported by multiple women, male colleagues had pulled me aside to tell me that they never had any problem with the student. ("Of course not," I answered each. "You're a man.")

Mostly the revisions to the essay are a conciliatory gesture, an olive branch that I'm willing to extend because I don't want harm to come to the student in this essay. I *am* sorry his feelings were hurt. Malice and vindictiveness are hateful motivations, and that's not why I write.

This essay was never really about him; our hallway conversation was only its trigger. The essay is about me. Or, more broadly, it is about language and community and an evolution I was witnessing and how we participate in shaping linguistic evolution.

Sometimes I wonder if the student asked for any sanctions. In calling, he may have questioned my suitability as a professor. He might even have suggested that the university consider my removal, though I suspect that someone as intelligent and soft spoken and polite as this student stopped short of making specific requests as to what kind of censure the university might exact. In any event, perhaps he was disappointed that I was only spoken to, or perhaps this was all he wished, for me to be silenced.

Yet my pledge in this essay was to speak, and speak I will. I once hurt his feelings unknowingly, but I can't plead ignorance if this essay hurts his feelings a second time. Rather, I can only say that I have weighed the potential for harm against the potential for good, and I hope the scales tip toward good.

By publishing this essay again, I have likely joined the list of cunt professors in this student's taxonomy. His context, perhaps the common context, remains different from my context. And yet, I'm willing to own this label under another, not uncommon definition, that of a woman who shares her thoughts and asks the questions she's been told to stop asking.

I Am Woman

One of my earliest memories is of a protest march in Athens, Ohio. I am perhaps four or five years old, and while my little sister rides in an army green backpack carrier, I am walking, and tired of walking, at my mother's side.

But we're not just *walking*. Together, we are marching—marching for equal rights. Even then, I understand that this distinction matters. My mother believes that this day, this action, will affect my future. She is a member of the League of Women Voters, and they have organized this march. ERA NOW proclaim the bold blue buttons on every woman's chest. Our town is hilly and my legs ache and I don't want to march or walk or move. "This is important," my mother tells me. "We have to keep going."

I got my first stereo after I got my first job. I was seventeen and the guys I worked with called me Biscuit Babe and Hot Pan, shouting for more trays as we worked our early morning shift at Hardee's. The job paid minimum wage, $4.25 an hour, but a few months' savings allowed me to order from a JCPenney catalog a stereo that contained CD, dual cassette, and record players. In my car I played Nirvana, Pearl Jam, and Alice in Chains, but at home I raided my parents' stack of long unplayed LPs, taking the *Best of the British Blues* (John Mayall, Eric Clapton), the Rolling Stones' *Big Hits Volumes I and II*, Big Brother and the Holding Company's *Cheap Thrills*, the Beatles' White Album, and Helen Reddy's *I Am Woman*. Late into the night, I would play them in turn, setting out cards for solitaire as I sat in front of the speakers, absorbing.

When people in my family say I have a good memory, what they mean is, I supply the details. I hold the word "remember" in question. I suspect the details are largely inserted by imagination. Even so, I tend to be right about the broad strokes. The ERA march is a fact as well as a memory. The stereo had a laminated fake oak cabinet, where the records leaned like smokers in an alley.

I've heard people complain that Reddy's one-hit wonder is too soft and lyrical. It's not *forceful*, they say, under which I hear, it's not *masculine*. "I Am Woman" is a distinctly female anthem. It doesn't shriek or rant. It doesn't demand. It doesn't shove or hit or proclaim. Reddy's song calmly and lyrically states facts: she is strong; she is wise; she is invincible. These things are as inarguable as a brook or a sky or a songbird.

I sometimes teach literature surveys in which I give slide-show-based lectures summarizing the historical movements of each era corresponding to our Norton anthologies. When we reach the twentieth century, I ask my class, "When did the U.S. Congress pass the Equal Rights Amendment for women?"

They usually stare back, unsure. We are in territory the history books didn't cover.

"I'll give you a hint," I say. "The Fourteenth and Fifteenth Amendments, which granted equal rights to men born or naturalized into the United States regardless of race or skin color, were ratified in 1870."

My students guess the women's rights must have passed in 1890, 1900.

"I'll give you another hint," I say. "Women got the right to vote in 1920, and the ERA was proposed in 1923."

My students guess the 1930s, the 1940s.

"OK, last hint," I say. "The Civil Rights Act passed in 1964."

They guess the 1960s, the 1970s, the 1980s.

"Tell us," they say. "Tell us when it passed."

Even in her depiction of strength, Reddy uses distinctly female imagery, invoking birth itself. Her wisdom is born of pain; she is still an embryo. Childbirth is the benchmark of physical pain, yet when creating icons of strength, popular culture conjures men like Rocky or Rambo. Mothers are low on the list, associated instead with home and love. Only when dressed in the trappings of those tough guys, as Sarah Connor was in *Terminator 2: Judgment Day*, are they able to transcend. In the American imagination, mothers are where we turn when we feel vulnerable. They are places of safety rather than strength.

Reddy suggests they can be both.

The light scratching on my mother's record created a warmth each time I played her records, a kind of sonic hug. As it spun, it was as if she wrapped her arms around me and lifted me to her hip. It was as if it said, tired as we might be, we have to stand, to march. We would support each other and move forward.

It never passed, the ERA. Not at the national level. Any equality that women have has been fought for in court, not written into law by the United States Congress. Any equality we have is fragile. Any equality we have is not actually equality at all.

The year 2016 was one of deaths: Elie Wiesel, Muhammad Ali, Janet Reno, David Bowie, Alan Rickman, Harper Lee, Gene Wilder, Jim Harrison, William Trevor, Fidel Castro, Florence Henderson, Umberto Eco, John Glenn, Carrie Fisher, Prince.

My mother's death that March did not make any headlines. She left the world quietly.

Some songs take the world by its throat. Some drumbeats kick their listeners in the gut. Some guitars scream until you listen. Some singers growl, some shout, some taunt, some plead, some rant. For most of my life, I gravitated toward those singers, thrashing my way through metal and grunge. Helen Reddy was an exception. Her anthem, pulled from my mother's collection, makes me go still, reminding me that power can take different, more feminine forms.

Taking It to the Logo

What I remember: A rock band roadie bragging. He claims that he tests girls by the measure of a drumstick, asking them to insert it in their vagina to see if they can "take it to the logo." I watched him on a basement TV in a room of boys who laughed and laughed and laughed. "That's so sick," one said, but their laughter read less like condemnation, more like respect, awe, applause.

Twenty-six years later, I am racking my brain, asking it to give up more details. Which boys were in the room? What was the goal of inserting the stick? To get backstage? To meet the band? What was the video? Who was the band? I post what I remember on Twitter, asking for leads, but no one seems to know what I'm talking about. The memory of the video seems mine alone.

I wonder if perhaps the clip was from a Metallica rockumentary, but that doesn't seem right. The drumstick roadie seems more likely to be from the world of glam rockers and hair bands, the groups for whom women were nothing more than ever-present accessories, the groups who couldn't make an album cover without a half-naked lady flung over a car hood, the groups whose videos featured band members dripping with girls who licked and petted them as they tried to drive, or play their instruments, or live their lives. Metallica had always had a different focus: less sex, more fury.

I've thought about this roadie many times in the subsequent decades, but lately he's become a daily thought. The Kavanaugh hearings are on, and in the wake of Weinstein, as we wrestle once again with perennial questions about whether women are really people, the entertainment that has always been part of my life provokes reflections on rock and roll, exploitation, and celebrity. "When you're a star," Donald Trump said as he bragged about sexual assault, "they let you do it. You can do anything." I've thought about the "they" in this sentence, wondering whether this vague pronoun is meant to denote the women themselves or the passive people who witnessed or the nation as a whole and its silent complicity. I wonder about our creation of icons. I wonder about sex as a motivator for stardom. I watch how stories of silence and "implied consent" are used to rewrite assault as something more benign. Mostly, though, I'm thinking about laughter.

> Indelible in the hippocampus is the laughter, the laugh—the uproarious laughter between the two, and their having fun at my expense.

> I was, you know, underneath one of them while the two laughed, two friend—two friends having a really good time with one another.

> the laughter, the uproarious laughter, and the multiple attempts to escape, and the final ability to do so.

> —Christine Blasey Ford, excerpts from the Kavanaugh hearing transcript

I went hunting for the clip to test my memory, to prove or disprove what I thought I knew. I googled phrases, looked for video transcripts, and came up short. I tried to think of other bands, other documentaries. I turned again to Metallica, only it couldn't be Metallica, could it? Vince Neil, Bret Michaels, Axl Rose—those guys specialized in looking indifferent/annoyed as women, seemingly unable to help themselves, ran fingers through the singers' feathered hair. James Hetfield of Metallica was something else. He sunk into his thighs when he played, centering himself, weight in his feet, like a man prepared to take a hit and return one. He wore his guitar slung low, as if to block crotch shots, and belted lyrics from the gut, the words slugging out—jab, jab, uppercut, hook. His singing wasn't there to prettify; rather, his voice roughed up the guitar a little, lacing growl in with melody. It wasn't a woman-friendly band exactly, but Metallica gave voice to a rage that resonated with me. They seemed more ally than enemy. Even so, my mind kept turning back to them. It couldn't be, but if not them, then who?

In the days before the 90th Academy Awards, street artists Plastic Jesus and Joshua "Ginger" Monroe created a golden statue of Harvey Weinstein sitting robed on his casting couch. "Everyone wants a selfie, everyone wants to be part of the experience," Ginger is quoted as saying in a *Hollywood Reporter* article discussing the statue. "To be able to knock the monster down a peg and poke fun and ridicule it helps remove its power. That's how you take these powerful people down. As Mark Twain once said, 'Against the assault of laughter, nothing can stand.'"

They seem to assume that their art has accomplished this assault, this victory. They assume the casting couch has imploded under the weight of laughter.

What I remembered most of *A Year and a Half in the Life of Metallica* was its length: two full VHS tapes of mostly dull footage of studio recordings and concerts in support of their sixth CD, the self-titled release we simply called the Black Album, the one that finally launched them to fame. Of course I had owned *A Year and a Half*. Metallica had been my first rock concert. In 1992 I owned every CD, knew every lyric, could recite details of every band member, living and dead, but even then I couldn't bring myself to love the documentary. I had long ago relegated it to a donation pile, a relic of my past.

The miracle and curse of the Internet, though, is that pasts don't disappear. YouTube supplied what I had discarded. Better still, I could control its speed, bumping the footage up to time and a half, chipmunk metal heads racing through their riffs.

> Fowley invited other guys to have sex with Jackie before removing his own pants and climbing on top of her. "Kim's fucking someone!" a voice shouted from the door of the motel room to the partygoers outside, calling them in to watch. Arguelles returned to the room to see if this was all a big joke.
>
> On the bed, Fowley played to the crowd, gnashing his teeth and growling like a dog as he raped Jackie. He got up at one point to strut around the room before returning to Jackie's body.
>
> —Jason Cherkis, "The Lost Girls: One Famous Band, One Huge Secret, Many Lives Destroyed," *Huffington Post*

I'm midway through footage from what had been the second tape when I see him: the roadie, just as I remembered. Or not *just*. He's a little younger, a little leaner. His name is Eddy or Eddie, perhaps like Van Halen's famous lead guitar, perhaps like Iron Maiden's cover ghoul, perhaps like water swirling in place. He works on the sound crew—"I fly the P.A.," he says. He calls the area below stage the Underworld and welcomes us in.

Immediately, he's talking about girls, flipping through Polaroid after Polaroid, the trophies he's kept from each conquest. "I figure, if they can take the stick up to the logo," he says, "they get to keep the stick. If not, they've got to give it back and try again."

I stop the video and back it up. I slow it now to three-quarter time. Taking it to the logo isn't a ticket to meet the band, as I thought. Taking it to the logo wins them only the stick. I get trapped in the impossibility of the final sentence, how one must both give it back and try again, two things you can't do simultaneously. I think of bacteria, of pain, of our soft insides, of the danger of penetration.

Eddie has moved on. He brags about the mother he fucked so her daughter could get backstage. He insists she would have done anything, and "Me, being the type of guy I am, asked 'em and they said yeah." He flips to another photo, another girl. "This one here, she was a trouper. Everybody shot a wad on her—I mean, in the crew." He refers to one after another as a "nice girl." Nice, for Eddie, means compliant.

At my husband's office, the receptionist is flashed by a man outside the plate glass window. She's shaken. She reports the incident. "Just laugh at it," one of the male bosses advises. "He wants a response. Don't give it to him." She can take control over the situation, her boss insists, and take the flasher's power away, as if her laughter could erase the act itself.

I can't make this logic work. I try to extend it: If a woman laughs at assault, is it no longer assault? If she laughs during rape, is it no longer rape? Exactly how does this give her power? She has substituted the response suggested by one man's actions with the response suggested by another man's words. Nothing changes the assault itself.

Refusing a man's delight is the power historically assigned to women going back to *Lysistrata*, but refusal is not the same as power. It makes nothing happen, nothing change. It cannot instigate. It cannot create.

"Laugh at him," a man advises, and his advice is kindly meant. The boss is, in fact, a wonderful and warm human being who tries to make the world—or, at least, the world of their office—a better place. He imagines himself in the receptionist's chair, but he has forgotten to check and stow his male confidence, his physical presence, his power. There is no way for a woman visually assaulted at a window to not be visually assaulted at a window, regardless of how she responds. Her reaction is hers alone—to look away, to laugh, to report, to cringe, to vomit, to gossip, to relive and relive and relive, to know that any moment the man may be back at the window, to know that he might not stay at the window, to know that, if he charges in, nothing will stop him in time to help her.

Here's another thing I didn't remember: Eddie's return to the video. In what is now minute 14 of part 7 of part 2 in the series of self-perpetuating YouTube clips, he's onscreen and the band is watching his footage. Kirk Hammett jokes about how this video is launching Eddie's career, their roadie having his moment of celebrity. Lars Ulrich, the drummer, is red-faced with laughter next to a grinning Jason Newsted as Eddie flips through the photos of girls he's fucked under their stage. Kirk Hammett is laughing too, but as Eddie's monologue hits the drumstick test, the video cuts to Kirk exiting the room. He scowls back at the camera as he shoves the door open, a man on a mission. He throws a wad of something at a kind of shed door in the bowels of the arena. It all feels a little staged.

The footage cuts to three girls outside, sweaty but self-confident. "We're trying to get backstage," they say, "but we're not having any luck because the roadies are being assholes." Another cuts in, "They want favors." Another, maybe the first, says, "They want a blowjob for a backstage pass." The girls and the roadies are both out of luck. "We're not going to degrade ourselves like that," the girls say.

That's the word: degrade. They were asked and they refused. They had a choice, and they stayed classy. I hear the subtext whispering that all of this has been consensual. The girls whom Eddie fucked were fucked because they allowed it. It's not rape but sex. And I suppose it is, depending on your definition of consent and of assault, depending on how you want to weigh celebrity and power, depending on whether age matters, depending on whether you mind the *need* ringing in the voice of the loveless girl in another part of the video, recounting her life of being "locked up," of floating from foster home to foster home until no one wanted her anymore, depending on whether you view a girl exchanging sex for a backstage pass as a kind of assault or prostitution or simply an opportunity for someone to meet their favorite band.

We're back to Kirk, a shirtless Eddie at his side. Eddie says, "I'm not going to go into any post offices with my gun anymore."

"That's good." Kirk nods. "That's a positive step forward. I like that. I like that."

"No more wiping people out at McDonald's."

"I like that, too," Kirk says, but his eyes are darting around.

In between the lines, I imagine I am supposed to see a moral lesson having been imparted, but the violence being sworn off is not the violence he has committed. We feel Eddie's tongue in his cheek, his performance designed to evoke laughter once again. His response is to joke. Though I can't confirm this, he appears to have kept his job on the sound crew. I wonder how much of this footage is meant simply to make us feel that something's been done, even as we watch nothing being done.

The film rolls on. Before the documentary ends, we'll watch footage of girls flashing the camera alongside footage of a girl's bikini top pulled aside by someone near her, as if the girl's consent was never an issue because, let's face it, it never was.

The Guns N' Roses album *Appetite for Destruction* was named for the artwork that was to be its cover until retailers objected to the band's choice and refused to stock the album. In Robert Williams's graphic, a girl slumps against a wall, shirt open and naked breast exposed and cut, panties around her ankles. The image implicates a robot passerby as the perpetrator. We are, I suppose, to forgive the band for their choice in art, relegated to the inner sleeve of the record or tape or CD, and for the subsequent promotional art in which the robot boozes or barbecues, aligning the rapist/robot with the band, and for the concert t-shirts that omit the robot altogether and show only the raped girl, the words "Guns-N-Roses Was Here" graffitied on the wall behind her. It's all in good fun.

From 1981 to 1994, Lars Ulrich played with Calato Regal Tip sticks, size 5B. These are the sticks Eddie would have had in stock. Searching online,

I learn they are sixteen inches long. The logo is just shy of halfway down the stick.

How much counted as taking it "to the logo"? Six inches? Seven? It's not an impossible length, but rather a test of their willingness. Were the sticks he offered dirty or clean? How dull or sharp was that nylon tip? Were the ends already wrapped, performance ready? How easily did they splinter? How easily did they break? What did Eddie do with the sticks from the girls who failed his metric?

> Both the Kavanaugh accusations share certain features: There is no penetrative sex, there are always male onlookers, and, most importantly, there's *laughter*. In each case the other men—not the woman—seem to be Kavanaugh's true intended audience. In each story, the cruel and bizarre act the woman describes—restraining Christine Blasey Ford and attempting to remove her clothes in her allegation, and in Deborah Ramirez's, putting his penis in front of her face—seems to have been done in the clumsy and even manic pursuit of male approval.
>
> —Lili Loofbourow, "Brett Kavanaugh and the Cruelty of Male Bonding," *Slate*, 25 September 2018

When I read about assault, when I write about it, I take a killjoy's stance. The truth is, I love to laugh. Laughter is contagious, human, fun. Laughter brings us together and solidifies our sociality, confirming us as part of a group, as friends. Laughter can be an instrument of change. With it, we acknowledge absurdity and contradiction.

I know, too, that laughter can be an instrument to silence and shut down. Good things are not always good.

I wonder where Eddie is now. More than a quarter of a century since the Black Album, Eddie has surely moved on to some other job. We have shamed so many celebrities, but I see them returning quietly to their work. Kavanaugh has been confirmed to the Supreme Court. The country has delivered a verdict.

I, too, have laughed at inappropriate times: the news of a friend's death, the attack on the Twin Towers. I heard in my laughter the tinge of panic, the completeness of my ignorance of how to respond, and the horror at what my body was doing in the vacuum of that knowledge. That sound was not the sound of the boys' laughter as we watched the video, nor is it the sound of Lars Ulrich's or Kirk Hammett's or Jason Newsted's laughter. In all that male laughter, what I hear first is delight. The laughter acknowledges that a man is behaving badly, but it seems to me I can also hear the appreciation of his daring, just as they appreciate The Who for destroying hotel rooms, only in this case it is a person who is being destroyed, or who is resisting being destroyed.

What do I do with the music I grew up with? I turned to it once because it contained the rage I felt, but now I can't unhear its complicity in so much of what I rage against. It taps against my eardrum, its pitch lower than the bass. In "sex, drugs, and rock and roll," the sex always comes first. Rock and roll is the means to an end, and that end is permission to behave badly and fuck broadly. In my own professional community, male writers are being outed for their sexual crimes with students and other aspiring writers on our own version of the casting couch, but most are quietly forgiven or loudly defended on social media. It seems to have always been the deal—if you're a star, you get away with it. They let you. "They" meaning us.

The boys I watched with laughed because they could, because they were more aligned with Eddie than they were with the girls in the photographs. I sat silent, absorbing. I knew I should smile; that is the rule. To do otherwise would make me a downer. I wish I could remember whether I forced my lips to curl.

I have never been raped. My first boss used to rub his body against my backside while I rolled out biscuit dough for the morning rush, no matter how often I told him to knock it off. I've been catcalled and whistled at more times than I can count. On at least two occasions while I was running, strange men have asked me to get in their cars so that I could "give them directions." Even after I became a professor, a male colleague used to regularly stand in my door and vigorously rub his penis through the pocket of his pants as he spoke to me on another invented pretext. But I have never been raped. I am lucky.

Victory Tischler-Blue was Jackie's replacement on bass, and one of her main memories from her time as a Runaway was how some of the other members made fun of what happened to Jackie. "I heard about that nonstop," she says now. "They would talk about Kim fucking Jackie like a dog. It was kind of a running joke."

Oftentimes during soundchecks, Tischler-Blue says that Smythe would play his secret recording of Jackie's breakdown in Japan. He made listening to it part of the band's pre-show ritual. "He was taunting her and she started screaming, 'I'm sick of being sick,'" Tischler-Blue remembers. "It became a catchphrase with the band. She was shrieking it. It shook me to my core—and everybody would laugh."

—Cherkis, "The Lost Girls"

The experience of watching a roadie brag onscreen is not remotely on par with the experience of a woman surviving attempted rape, yet in the topography of small assaults we may sometimes trace the topography of large assaults.

As a nineteen-year-old girl, I bought a documentary. There's a perfect length for everything; this was not that length. Even in the height of my fandom, the two VHS cassettes were too long. They could have cut many things: the reckless car rides, the stripper in the studio, the band members on couches flipping through porn. They could have cut Eddie. Because they did not, a truth was caught on camera. Of course, we all knew the mythology of roadies, and rock bands themselves have never been shy about their love of sexual gratification. I knew that high school guys picked up guitars in the hope that they could become gods, and that sometimes this fantasy came true. Their success was measured in women. Their crimes were masked in laughter.

Twenty-some years later, I know the drumstick penetrated; I took it inside me, stabbing straight up through the vagina and into the heart of my matter. It lodged. It has long ago ossified into vestigial bone. If I laugh now, I will choke on it.

Evening

Super Bowl XLVIII

Even at odds, my mom and I agree on this: 2014 is the Seahawks' year. This doesn't diminish the distance across the couch.

My friends insist football is brutal and inhuman. They cite CTE, date rape, suicide and murder, the sport itself, and I agree and agree and agree. Yet here I am, sitting in a curtained room as the evening flicker of the game strobes the descending dark.

I know brain damage. Over the past few years, my mother's once silent stroke has revealed itself. Her memory continues its ebb. She cannot now remember where she left her keys, her car, her house. She forgets how long to bake a potato; she leaves the bacon on high even as it billows smoke. She forgets how many times (too many) she's filled her wine glass, forgets to close doors and drawers and cabinets, forgets that she should keep her clothes on—in front of her grandchildren and in front of the neighbors.

The odds are against her. Her sharp brown eyes, once as cutting as the Seahawks' keen green, have hazed past the horizon. She grew up in Philly. In her twenties, she held Eagles season tickets and, with her six younger brothers, loved and cheered the team. Ask and my uncles will tell you how Dolphins once swam away with a season, about broken quarterbacks and too short quarterbacks, cheapass owners and shithole stadiums. Their memories are long and comprehensive, as hers once was. Now, she has lost even the down. She asks which team has possession, what quarter we're in. The lacing's all undone, the spiral unbound.

Fourth and ten. Once again I'm punting terse answers, the old habit I loathe myself for. She's gone a distance I fear I'll follow. She deserves better from me, especially now.

Then, in a dizzying moment, she returns with Flutie's Hail Mary, with Theisman's break, with the offensive line of the '75 Steelers, with Unitas, Montana, Starr, Brown, Greene, Largent. She runs on, rattling off a hundred old moments safeguarded somewhere against time's terrible taking tide. And moored among the memories is my childhood, the love I gave, and how, in my teens, that love warped, bending into something weird and ugly, yet love all the same.

The score between us? Tally the times I called her stupid against the times she said I didn't hug her back. Tally the times she left me waiting on a curb, unsure if she would ever arrive. Tally the hated flute I played at her insistence. Tally the barn owner she paid so that I could ride, and the overtime she worked, and my long, latchkey afternoons. Tally her hopes for me and also her expectations. Tally our old arguments, the long-rehearsed words we barked at one another. Tally our history of unremarkable failures and how they added up against each other. All that we did and didn't: strike the marks. I can't forgive her, and I can't thank her enough.

Once it seemed I couldn't win. Now she's forgotten to fight. It disarms and disorients me. We argued until argument defined us, as if we'd always been destined to face off from opposite sides of ever-moving imagined lines. I don't know who we are now. I can't calculate the time we have left, ticking, or the distance now still between us, or the love, malformed but enormous. Always at odds, we can't find an evening, even as this bleak darkness descends. I don't yet know that, in the year after her death, her Eagles will hoist the championship trophy themselves, or how I will both thrill and ache, wishing she could see it.

For now, I am trapped in this inescapable night. My children are too young to lose a grandmother to dementia, but there is no flag for this unfairness. We watch a game that beats on tough men's skulls. The brain, too, is a body part, but it does not repair itself. Her mind and theirs will not reknit like a broken bone or pop into place after dislocation.

The clock's count relentless, I loft a pass, a hand stretched to hers as we watch the game.

The Gun That Won the West

Let's not pretend I was an unbiased researcher. I had intentions. I had best laid my plans. I set out to write an essay about guns and guilt and the female body. That's the story I'd first encountered all those years ago while watching a random episode of A&E's *America's Castles*. The legend lodged in me, building a little home in which to live, paying little board. As I recall, it went like this:

A widow and heiress, consumed by grief at the loss of her husband and infant daughter, consults a Boston medium. He identifies the source of her bad luck: she's haunted by those killed by the Winchester repeating rifle, the gun that won the West, the sale of which had made her fortune. She sought escape in motion, moving from Connecticut to California. She bought a house and hired laborers to construct elaborate traps and tricks to fool the phantoms who pursued her. The house, that icon of Victorian womanhood, became the receptacle and representation of all her torment. She constantly devised new wings, custom-ordered glass, designed everything from stairwells to faucets. Building continued twenty-four hours a day, 365 days a year, until her death. In effect, she had scapegoated herself, shouldering her country's shame like a heavy woolen mantle. She fled directly into her own madness and transmuted guilt into architecture.

How could I not be fascinated? Ghostlike, she's haunted me all these years, until finally I began in earnest to research and write. Her story was perfect as a plum, weighty and dripping with juice. The problem, I would learn, was that the story wasn't true.

1988: GUN #1

I was a fifteen-year-old white girl living in the booming Los Angeles sub-urbs amid the palm trees and pepper trees and orange groves of the Inland Empire. My school, Riverside Poly High, was called "the rich kids' school," though as one of our teachers snidely reminded us, if any of us were *really* rich, we would have been in private school. Still, we were generally do-ing well enough. Many of us had backyard pools. A lucky few got cars for their birthdays, including our future valedictorian, who had scored a white BMW complete with sunroof.

I had moved from small-town Ohio a few years earlier and lacked the fashion sense to know Gucci from Jordache. My parents' finances were comparatively limited, first from buying the house here and then from my mother's graduate school tuition, so for most of my childhood, my clothes came from the bargain basement—an unforgiveable sin in a nouveau-af-fluent neighborhood. Even so, I felt safe if not accepted.

If there's one thing rich kids' schools specialize in, it's cultivating out-siders. Looking back, it's easy to recognize the kid who sat behind me in U.S. History as just another reject, like me. If I didn't recognize him as one, it was only because he wasn't on my radar at all. He was quiet. I don't remember even being aware of him behind me each day until the day he nudged me before class, opening his school bag and inviting me to look inside.

I remember the backpack as an oily blue, the gun itself as chrome and shining. I don't remember him saying anything. I don't remember speak-ing either. The situation, more than anything, confused me. Why the need to show the gun? Why to me? In those pre-Columbine years, I didn't ex-actly feel threatened, but I knew the gun had no place in that classroom. I didn't speak. I shrugged it off.

STATES

The gun debate in this country is dominated by two factions holding dis-parate sets of beliefs. Pro-Gun: I love guns and everyone should have one. Anti-Gun: I don't like guns and no one should have one. The Pro-Gun faction believes the world will be safer only when everyone is armed. The Anti-Gun faction suggests that, if safety is what we want, we should melt the guns. Neither stance is productive. Neither side wants to be persuaded.

WINCHESTER

The widow may have moved west for any number of reasons. She and her late husband had traveled to the Bay Area years before, and she had loved her time there. More recently, her brother-in-law had taken a job at Stanford. Though she had grown up in modest circumstances, she was now a woman of means with the opportunity to direct her own life. She didn't travel alone, but brought several family members. The house that is now the Winchester Mystery House was only one of the properties she would buy in the area.

From the outside, the mansion looks only beautiful. The squarely trimmed hedgerows, the manicured palms, even the controlled profusion of the blooming flowerbeds suggest more order than chaos. The grass, trimmed and uniformly green, spreads like a blanket. She chose a sunny mustard color for the house, trimmed with olive and capped with red tile, everything tasteful. Even the Victorian gingerbread, with the regularity of machine-cut shingles and trim, suggests a measured and regular mind. So convincing is the appearance of normality that the caretakers have had to label the door to nowhere. Otherwise you might miss it and step into the void.

So much mythology surrounds the house and its owner that it is difficult to disentangle fact from fiction. We know she married William Wirt Winchester, son of Oliver Winchester and heir to the Winchester Repeating Arms Company, and that they lived in New Haven and that they had a daughter who died forty days after her birth. Many years later, William died at age forty-three of tuberculosis. In the wake of this second loss, Sarah continued to keep homes on Prospect Street, though New Haven city registries would eventually note that she "removed to Europe." A full three years passed before she moved west, bought a house in San Jose, California, and began her famous construction project.

In 2017 and 2018, as I was researching this essay, the Winchester Mystery House website (where, conveniently, you could buy tickets for the

Mansion Tour, the Explore More Tour, the Friday the 13th Flashlight Tour, and the Hallowe'en Candlelight tour) portrayed Sarah Winchester as "a true woman of independence, drive, and courage who lives on in legend as a grieving widow who continuously built (and built and built) onto her initially small, two-story farmhouse to appease the spirits of those killed by the guns manufactured by her husband's firearms company."

It is true that, like many women of her day, Sarah believed in spiritualism. She held séances, hoping to commune with the dead. Yet historians have found no evidence of the Boston psychic who was said to have prompted her journey west. The mythology says that she was grief-stricken, but it had been several years since her husband's death and almost two decades since she'd lost her daughter. There is no time limit on grief, of course, but if we're to believe that she fled in the wake of loss, it took some time for her grief to coalesce into action.

1989: GUN #2

We moved to Moscow, Idaho, the summer before I turned sixteen. When I started school, I saw everyone in types. The names were new, the hairstyles and clothing slightly different, but what struck me was how each person I met had a corollary person whom I'd known in California: the thin, upright girl with ironed jeans and slender fingers earning top marks in every class; the smiling jock pretending to know less than he did as he dandled a bouncing pencil from his fingertips in Calculus. I knew them all. I just had to learn the names of these new, particular Idaho versions.

The ten-year-old boy on the bus was, at first, an exception. He got on five or six stops after me at a little green farmhouse, always wearing a beaten leather biker jacket and a scowl framed by dirty blond hair. I'd never before seen a child look so fiercely and continually angry. I said something to that effect one day as I was getting off at the high school with my classmate, who told me the story: He used to smile, she said. Two years before, though, he had found his father's gun and it went off. He killed his brother. An eight-year-old murderer. An accident. A mistake.

Even then, I recognized it as a common story.

She may not have intended to martyr herself, but the myth of her exile and relentless self-punishment has proved lucrative. The 2017 version of the Winchester Mystery House website boasted: "Since 1923 the story of Sarah Winchester and her incredibly peculiar house has fascinated more than 12 million people from around the world who have toured its lonely hallways, dark passages and ornate rooms." Many more have visited since. As a nation, we've invested heavily in her myth, funding tour after tour. The museum has added attractions over the years, including "Sarah's Attic Shooting Gallery." Of it they wrote, "In the seemingly unending lore and physical labyrinth that is the Winchester Mystery House an entirely new room was recently 'discovered' (wink, wink) and is now open for guests to experience."

Winchester rifles adorned the website, alongside white-eyed specters in Victorian dress who promise ghostly activity in this gaily painted haunted house. The site advertised *Winchester*, the 2018 horror movie starring Helen Mirren as Sarah Winchester and repeated the popular claim that "After the sudden deaths of her husband and child, she threw herself into the 24-hours a day, seven days a week construction of an enormous mansion designed to keep the evil spirits at bay," though we know that neither death was sudden, that years separated these events, and that the records uncovered by Mary Jo Ignoffo in her 2010 biography *Captive of the Labyrinth* show that Winchester dismissed workers for months at a time, proving that the work was hardly constant.

The Winchester House website highlighted the house's repeated use of the number thirteen, signifying her supposed interest in the occult, but when Ignoffo investigated Winchester's alleged fondness for thirteen, she uncovered another explanation. James Perkins, a carpenter who'd worked for years on the Winchester home, asserted: "The number 13 in chandeliers, the number of bathrooms, windows, ceiling panels and other things were certainly put in after she died." Ignoffo notes that the chandelier with its thirteenth candle appears "poorly amended," out of keeping with Winchester's careful selection of impeccable pieces. Indeed,

Perkins "averred that 'the more irregular features, which have made the house a world-famous oddity, were built after Mrs. Winchester's death.'" Ignoffo continues, "The first mention of the use of the number thirteen in the Winchester house did not appear in print until 1929, and after that, Winchester's supposed obsession with thirteen is mentioned in almost every article."

Winchester Mystery House lore states that many of the architectural oddities have been attributed to Winchester's desire to fool and confuse the ghosts that she believed pursued her. Famous among these are the "stairs to nowhere" and doors that open to nothing. However, Ignoffo points out: "The house's so-called stairs that lead to nowhere had previously led to an upper floor. Likewise, the doors that now open out into thin air were once entryways to suites of rooms, and pipes protruding from the house's exterior once plumbed upper floors. The oddities of the giant house are easily understood when one takes into account the massive earthquake of 1906." That quake not only destroyed many parts of Winchester's house, but it also damaged her confidence in herself. As Ignoffo puts it, "Winchester was forced to confront her own limitations as an architect, and she was not very forgiving. Her designs, instructions, and careful plans did not hold up against natural forces." She sealed herself from the sight of her failure, a psychological explanation less likely to sell tickets.

Visit the Winchester Mystery House website now, and you will find a site vastly different from the one I saw in 2017, though the old site is accessible using Wayback Machine Internet Archive for those who are curious. The new site is slick, dominated by footage that pans across a stately home and garden. Sarah's Attic Shooting Gallery has been replaced by less on-brand axe throwing, in keeping with modern trends. The site promotes the estate as a venue for weddings and team building events. Yet not all the ghosts of the past have been exorcised. The website continues to highlight After Dark and Halloween tours, boasts of a forthcoming Houdini-themed escape room, and implores guests to "never miss a mysterious moment." Like a remodeled home, the renovated website better aligns with our changing tastes, yet the original structure of the Sarah Winchester mythology maintains its shape. How much "wink, wink" has been involved in the marketing of the Winchester Mystery House? How much remains?

LITANY

Orlando. Virginia Tech. San Bernardino. The University of Texas clock tower. Dallas. Columbine. Sandy Hook.

1993: GUN #3

In my sophomore year of college, I met an old friend who asked if I had heard the news about a guy who'd gone to our small Idaho high school— I'll call him Joe. I was less close to him than my friends were, but he was a kind, steady guy, an Eagle Scout, with whom we'd joked and eaten our lunches each day. He was a couple years younger than we were, but he was part of our circle. I'd lost touch since graduation.

Joe, my friend now told me, had been hunting with his father when one of his shots sailed wide of a doe. They were wearing bright clothing, properly attired for safe hunting, but his father was concealed by foliage. Joe's shot killed his father instantly.

I should have asked for his number. I should have reached out. I didn't. I was nineteen years old, and I did not know what to say. I still don't know. What do you say to an eighteen-year-old kid who has just committed accidental patricide?

STATES

The *Washington Post* keeps a database of the number of people shot by police in a year. As I began drafting this essay in mid-July of 2017, the number was 543, and news was rolling in that police had shot and killed a forty-year-old white yoga teacher named Justine Diamond in Minneapolis. She had called them there herself, suspecting that a sexual assault was happening near her home.

I wonder if police would be so quick to draw if they didn't fear that everyone around them was armed. I suspect that they wouldn't. I suspect that the kill-or-be-kill mentality underlies too many of these calls, especially those in lower-income neighborhoods and those involving people of color. Belief and adrenaline too easily subvert fact.

1996: GUN #4

I moved to Oceanside, California, after graduation and took a job substitute teaching in the spring of the following year. The shooting at the high school happened on a day I was teaching elsewhere—maybe the junior high or an elementary school. The papers speculated whether the shooting was gang-related or drug-related, the usual explanations. Americans seem to expect school shootings in urban high schools. I returned to Oceanside High School to teach the following week. Nothing had changed. It was as though no one had been shot.

WINCHESTER

When I first heard the Sarah Winchester myth, I saw in her an artist. Having learned the facts and the fiction, I stand by that assessment. The house is an incredible creative act, entangled by legend. The two have grown together, like ivy into brick, and formed a structure worth investigating.

For Victorian women, the house was an area in which they could exert authority, so it makes sense to me that Sarah Winchester's solitary years were invested there, but architecture wasn't really seen as a woman's domain. As Christine R. Junker writes in "Unruly Women and Their Crazy Houses," Winchester "departed from gender norms because rather than showing interest in housekeeping, as a woman of her time should have, she was engaged in house *building*." She may have been a quiet little woman, but here she advocated for herself and her designs, using her lawyer like a sword to defend them from those who challenged her rights.

Junker argues that "the haunted house narrative obscures the much more interesting proposition that Winchester's house was built to satisfy her own creative and intellectual interests, an idea that certainly would have been—and can be read as—radical for her time: though she would have identified herself with the Victorian ideals of her childhood, it should be noted that her actions were more in keeping with the notion of radical material feminists of that time, who were advocating for women to seek empowerment and agency through control of their own domestic spaces." Ultimately, the Mystery House, or Llanda Villa as Winchester herself named it, "represented a creative and artistic experience for Winchester," an experience to which few women of her time had access.

2009: GUN #5

I had completed my doctorate and taken my first professorship when it happened: Ben Teague, the beloved husband of one of the English professors, was shot and killed at a reception for the local community theater. In the immediate aftermath, none of us could make sense of this, not the faculty, not my classmates. I hadn't known him personally, but I knew what he meant. Ben, white-bearded and loving, was a Santa Claus–like figure for so many members of our department. Who would want to kill Ben?

Over days, we would learn that the gunman had been through a divorce, that he had two children, that he was jealous of his wife's new lover. We would learn, too, that he was also a University of Georgia professor, an endowed chair in the Department of Marketing who was described in a CNN article on the shooting as "a distinguished professor with a national reputation." When he came armed to the reception, Ben tried to talk him into reason, let him see that there was no need for violence.

We wouldn't know this until later. What we did know was that a gunman was on the loose and our neighborhood was on lockdown. Since Columbine and Virginia Tech, lockdown was now a thing we did, a drill we practiced at school and at home. Within ten blocks of my rented house, the man had murdered three people—his ex-wife, her boyfriend, and Ben—before fleeing to a field where he turned the gun on himself.

LITANY

Michael Brown. Trayvon Martin. Eric Garner. Ezell Ford. Tamir Rice. Sandra Bland.

WINCHESTER

There's no evidence that the widow felt guilt over those killed by the rifle that would supply her fortune, but the facts of Sarah Winchester's life never seemed to matter. Ignoffo says: "Toward the end of the 19th century, the American press began to seriously acknowledge the brutality used against American Indians, and the American conscience began to be bothered by Indian atrocities." The rifle had, by then, a broad history of violence, one that Oliver Winchester's great-great-great-granddaughter would recount for the *Guardian*: "The Winchester was deployed to kill Native Americans defending their historic lands—and yet they also used the rifle with devastating effect, most notably at General Custer's last stand. African Americans also embraced the Winchester as a defensive weapon in the bloody period after the civil war, in which lynching was common. 'A Winchester rifle should have a place of honour in every black home,' as the civil rights crusader Ida B Wells wrote in 1892. And so the Winchester was used for many different causes during a violent period." And yet, according to Ignoffo, "there is no evidence that Sarah herself felt guilty about the repeating rifle or earning money from it."

The guilt is our own. As Joni Tevis writes in her essay "What Looks Like Mad Disorder," "You can see anything you want in Sarah Winchester. Craft a story from what bits and scraps you know. Her house is the primary document left to show us who she was, and it's so easy to read it wrong."

Except she did leave other documents, if we choose to read them. By 1906, Winchester owned nearly a dozen homes in the San Jose area, and none of the others seem particularly peculiar; they offer nothing worth packaging for our consumption. We ignore her papers, the words of her friends testifying to her sanity and measured actions. We ignore the absence of remorse.

Whatever draws visitors to the Winchester Mystery House, it is not her reality. We have invested—quite literally—in the constructed mythology surrounding Winchester and her house through the purchase of ticket after ticket. It hardly seems coincidental that, in the wake of yet another round of mass shootings, Sarah Winchester's ghost was resurrected again, this time for the screen. According to *Variety*, CBS bought the film rights for $3.5 million and *Winchester* earned $615,000 on its opening night alone.

Tevis is right about Sarah Winchester. We craft our story out of hers, making of it what we want. It seems we need a scapegoat after all. Whether she felt it herself, Sarah Winchester's consuming guilt is convenient for the rest of us. She carries that burden so that we don't have to. We make her pay the price for our Manifest Destiny.

STATES

Though no one is lining up to ask my opinion, I think a lot about guns. For years I've tried to hold a reasonable position: regulate; allow guns for hunting and home security, provided they are kept secure; license users; hold gun owners responsible for firearms that are "lost or missing" so that fewer flood into criminal markets. I don't hunt or compete in trap shooting or visit gun ranges to practice hitting targets, but, away from the immediacy of gun deaths, I've defended the right to do any of these activities, provided that we put in place some kind of safety mechanisms. I wonder whether I should take a harder tack.

The National Rifle Association hasn't offered compromises. They shout, "Second Amendment," insisting on the right to bear arms, conveniently cutting the amendment's introduction, which specifies that those arms were to support a well-regulated militia. They ignore the fact that militia was the police force of early America (municipal police departments started to appear only in the 1830s) and that the guns our Founding Fathers had in mind were single-fire muskets. The NRA has obscured and mythologized the Second Amendment. As with Sarah Winchester, Americans have been asked to believe a story about ourselves that is convenient and political rather than accurate.

WINCHESTER

She's not the only scapegoat. We're very good at shifting blame, shifting guilt. We fill all sorts of entities. In the wake of any mass murder, it's what we do best. What about school security? What about the FBI—what happened to their background checks? What about violence in video games?

What about parents? What about teachers—why didn't more of them throw their bodies in the paths of bullets? It's Hollywood's fault. It's the fault of the mentally ill. It's the school's fault. It's the fault of Congress. There are so many others who can carry the burden of our anger and loss, allowing us to stay in perpetual inertia. I have been guilty of this myself. I've been guilty in this essay.

What makes Winchester's case interesting is the way her story lifts the debate out of the current moment, the way it mythologizes and warps actual genocide until it is transformed into nothing more than a ghost story. Sarah Winchester's life bore all the necessary elements: the house to haunt, the crazed widow, the dead, the dead, the dead.

2012: GUN #6

I moved to Utah to begin a new job at Weber State University. As on all public university campuses in Utah, students with a concealed carry permit are allowed to carry loaded guns. I was in the middle of my second year there when the student shot himself in the leg.

As I recall, he tripped coming down the steps in front of the library, though I cannot now find confirmation of this detail in any of the news articles. Instead they stress that, since he had a concealed carry permit, he was perfectly within his rights.

I know his is not the only gun on campus. On any given day there are likely to be dozens. I think about this when assigning grades. Like any professor, I have had students who have been unhappy with my assessment of their work. They're under a good deal of stress, anxious to keep their scholarships, to earn the grades likely to land them in successful careers, even to stay in school. I know how this kind of anxiety can change perceptions. I understand that stress can lead to a bad decision, and that a bad decision with a gun could mean the end of me.

WINCHESTER

If we look at her house not as a manifestation of madness but instead as a work of art, I wonder how it changes what we see. If the function of art is to help us to question and reflect, perhaps Winchester's house holds up a mirror. Perhaps we should look.

Sarah Winchester's house was a mess not because ghosts haunted her but because her architectural decisions were guided by whims and passions. She consulted few experts. She ignored reason. Her house is a metaphor, but not the one we've used it for.

LITANY

It's 2017, and I can't write this essay fast enough. Days after I think I've finished the draft, the news of Las Vegas rolls in: 58 dead, 851 injured. There's a shooting in Maryland, another in Colorado. Twenty-seven are killed in their church in Sutherland, Texas, and then another five in Rancho Tehama, California. I send the essay out again, and days later, seventeen children and teachers are dead at a high school in Parkland, Florida. I wake to their stories playing on my radio. I rage.

STATES

I am one small person living one small life. According to the common wisdom, as a middle-class white person, I should not have brushed up against much gun violence. My story is an average one: an American life riddled with bullets.

The mythology about gunmen in our country is that they are crazy or they are gangsters and thugs and drug addicts and dealers. The truth looks very different. In my life, they have been children and adults. They have been wealthy and middle class and struggling. They have been white far more often than not. They have been my neighbors. They have been my friends. Here's the thing, though: If they weren't, should it matter? Why are we so reluctant to protect every life in this country?

The same year I saw my first gun in a suburban California high school classroom, I was asked to memorize the only lines of literature I would ever be asked to memorize, these lines from John Donne's "Meditation XVII":

> No man is an island, entire of itself; every man is a piece of the continent, a part of the main. If a clod be washed away by the sea, Europe is the less, as well as if a promontory were, as well as if a manor of thy friend's or of thine own were: any man's death diminishes me, because I am involved in mankind, and therefore never send to know for whom the bells tolls; it tolls for thee.

Friends in other classes memorized lines from Shakespeare or Wordsworth or Whitman or Poe. My teacher, Jeffrey Rice, chose these. I can't imagine selecting any more apt, more necessary for being alive in the current moment. Any man's death diminishes me. I am involved in mankind.

WINCHESTER

If William Wirt Winchester had been the one to live, if he, rather than his wife, went west and bought houses, if one of those houses were to have strange, discordant features, would anyone have noticed? The story of Eden is the story of Eve's guilt and repentance, not Adam's. Is there something particular about a woman's body, about our gendered expectations, that fit her for this work? Perhaps the question is irrelevant, but I still find myself thinking that Sarah was ideal: small, quiet, bereft. She was heir to a fortune amassed from gun sales, built on the graves. These exterior features mattered more than her interior truth. Her life was paper on which we wrote our story.

STATES

If the Winchester Mystery House is based on lies and inventions, so too is our national gun debate. We argue legend rather than fact. I won't pretend to know the solution to our current crisis, but I know this: If we're guided by research rather than mythos, we can find a better compromise. We must. Each day costs too many lives.

The America we live in is the result of constant remodeling, amending, reconstructing. So many states have been added since our Constitution was first authored. Territories have been divided as large rooms might be broken into small. The laws have changed to reflect the people. If we look around our country and dislike what we see, we change it.

If a part of a house becomes damaged or dangerous, we can do better than to wall it off, as Sarah Winchester did with the earthquake-damaged wing of her home. We can do better than to fill it with false stories, as the current owners of her house have done. We can open the walls, expose the beams, fix what's broken. We can create something new and beautiful on the strength of the foundation.

Dislocated

I. AT THE TIME

I sit where I was flung, my body supported scarecrow-like on a fence rail. My senses are straw-filled, my vision and hearing blurred, fuzzing. Through the haze of white noise, I take inventory; I was riding, then flying, then propped here, against this strong fence.

I am in an indoor arena in a strange barn. Everything is surreal: the indoor dirt, my indoor flight, the cloudy darkness, the crashing static in my ears. My right arm rests on the lowest slat, casual, as if I was just relaxing here, waiting for a bus or a train.

I start again. Think riding, flying, propped. This all makes sense, more or less. There is cause and effect and order. What doesn't make sense is the way my legs are bent under me. The angles are not natural, my knees and ankles are all wrong.

I realize I am shaking.

There are feet coming, rushing to where I sit. Something in my shoulder is coming, too. Coming to. A pain that's just waking up, with stretches and yawns, a pain like a flame-colored lion shaking itself from sleep.

The running people ask if I'm OK. I don't know the answer to this question, so I ask them to pull my legs out from under me. I lean right, and they pull thighs and calves left and around until my legs are lying straight, two logs of legs. I can't feel them through the pins and needles, but they appear unbroken. The barn looks less cloudy now, and the static is quieting. Pieces of me are starting to send signals, flames racing under my skin.

"My back stings," I say. They lean me forward slightly, not enough to move my arm from the fence slat, but enough to lift the back of my shirt.

"You have one hell of a raspberry back there," I'm told.

It is a hot raspberry, then, burning and sugary. I feel in danger of becoming all burning. The raspberry heat spreads like fire, quickly consuming. My mind and my metaphors are mixing, so I try to concentrate on things that are real: the soft footing below me, the solidity of the strong wooden fence that's holding me. I must pull myself together and get back on. That's what riders do.

A curly-haired woman asks if I want something to drink. A Pepsi? I nod, not knowing if I want a drink, just wanting to give an answer.

I try telling myself that pain is imaginary. It's all in my head and nerve endings. It is not tangible like wood and dirt. It's a floating thing, an abstract noun. If I can just get my brain around it, I can control it, herd it into the back of my conscious so that I can think clearly.

My shoulder hurts. Something within, a ligament or tendon, is screaming a tea kettle scream. I think, shh, shh.

The people standing around me look down from impossible heights. How did they become so tall? I say, "I think my shoulder is either broken or dislocated." My voice is flat and even. Distant. I am not sure how my tongue made the words. My body is pieces, and they are working independently of one another.

A woman I don't know says, "If it was dislocated, you'd be crying your eyes out," which is such a strange thing to say, as if our eyes could be washed away from our body with the flood of their own tears. Her voice is gruff and matter of fact and brooks no argument. We are horse people. This is our language.

Somehow, my tongue makes more words, "It hurts pretty bad," in the same flat voice, a voice that sounds too thick. I don't care if they believe me. I'm not trying to make a case. I don't want to convince them. I want to convince myself that if I keep my voice steady and concentrate on real things, tangible things, dirt and fence, dirt and fence, I will not become all pain.

The curly-haired woman is back, handing me a soda can, putting it into the hand of my good arm. I wrap my fingers around it, sense the coolness of its metal. She puts one hand over mine, a warm thin hand, steadies the can and pops it open. As I lift it to my dry lips, my hand is shaking again. I almost spill.

The soda is sweet and cool; its bubbles fizz against my tongue. I am not usually a Pepsi drinker, but I've never tasted anything so good. I pour it in, imagine it flooding through me, like oil into a combustion engine, soothing and smoothing the running parts, allowing them to function as one whole again.

The fire in my back has settled; a slow burn; a broad, dim flame. But that fire has kindled something. In my shoulder, somewhere deep, between humerus, scapula, and clavicle, the scream I couldn't silence has transformed into an inferno.

The women peel back the collar of my shirt to peek under. I wince and look the other way, toward the guilty horse at the end of the arena staring back at me with soft, quiet eyes. The mare seems to pity me. She appears remorseful and sad; the stirrups hang limp by her side. This was our test ride. I was thinking of buying her until she bolted, until the reins meant nothing, until I realized we shared no language. A ex-track horse, she understood a rider's weight to mean one thing: run.

"We'll need to get you to the hospital," the women say.

I clear my throat and nod. The nod sends off a shower of sparks in my arm. Gritman is the nearest hospital; it is two towns away. Two towns and fifteen miles of rutted gravel road. I'm not sure how I'll ever leave this fence, the only thing that's propping me, my only support, my bones.

II. LOOKING BACK

In total, it would be three hours from the time I hit the fence until I arrived at the ER. I wouldn't see my shoulder until then. By the time I arrived, the roaring pain was so loud that it was all I could do not to roar myself. I held my right arm up with my left, trying to hold it as high and steady as the fence had, but failing. Every small movement, a millimeter here or there, was an agony.

The emergency room nurse refused to cut off my shirts, though I first asked and then begged her to. I was wearing three to combat the late winter Idaho cold: an undershirt, a long-sleeved tee, and a thick gray sweatshirt without much give. Prim and practical, she insisted I'd want them tomorrow. "I won't," I told her. They were old shirts, shirts to wear to a barn, shirts to get dirty in, but she worked each in turn up my torso and over my good arm, before pulling it gingerly over the screaming one.

Until that moment, I had never understood my bones, never thought about the framework that determined the shape of my body. Until then, I had understood that I had broad, straight shoulders, like my mother and her father, and that these shoulders were not just a body part but a contribution to my whole. If a friend were to spot me on the street even if I were turned away, he might recognize me by the shape and set of my shoulders, the way they fit into the rest of my body.

But now, instead of my usual shoulder, the one that was always there at the edge of my peripheral vision, there was a disturbing sag. What had looked so solid, the uppermost right corner of me, was now a drooping jellysack of skin. There was no corner of me anymore. The concrete fact of my body revealed itself to be an illusion.

They slid a needle under my skin to find the vein, and I slept while they x-rayed and made me whole again. Later the doctor would tell me that I dislocated my shoulder in the wrong direction. He doubted the tendons and ligaments would tighten enough to hold my bones in place. "If this pops out again," he warned, "you'll have to get it surgically pinned." I silently vowed I wouldn't tell when it did.

I learned, too, that "raspberry" was a nice way of saying that I had taken all the skin off of my lower back. The nurse gave me a thick antibacterial goop to slather on until the epidermis regrew. The elastic body wrap of the shoulder immobilizer would rub against my skinless back, electrifying it with pain for weeks. A full two years after the accident, the shadow of that fence rail still darkened my back where the skin regrew.

Decades later, it is a silly thing to be thinking of that day. As injuries go, a shoulder dislocation is banal, and within a few months I had the use of my shoulder again, though it would never again allow my arm to stretch in ways that were once easy.

Now I am prone to dislocating. At inconvenient times, perhaps serving a tennis ball or pulling down a heavy object, the bone of my arm will slide away from its home in my shoulder socket, sending out sparks from the embers of a fire that won't entirely extinguish.

Though the doctor had forewarned me of this proclivity for dislocation, what went unpredicted was my tendency, now, to run into door frames and walls, always and only with my right-hand shoulder, as if I have no idea anymore where the edges of myself reside. At one sickening glance at the dislocation, the map of my geography irrevocably shifted.

Before the accident, I would have said that the body made space for the mind and gave it home. Anatomical diagrams show the brain, its gray folds protected by bone. I understood synapses, the electricity of thought, sensation, movement, and emotion. But on the fence that day, my mind had cast its protective shroud. My own body, like the loam I sat in and the fence at my back, was a foreign thing.

I once thought of this as shock, but that's not correct. In medicine, it is called a vasovagal response. Extreme pain stimulates the vagus nerve (the tenth cranial nerve), resulting in a drop in both heart rate and blood pressure. Often this results in fainting or, as in my case, a sense of estrangement from oneself and the physical world. Radio static. Fog.

The science only goes so far, and I knock myself over and over against its rigid frameworks. On the fence, the dislocated body felt no pain. For fifteen, maybe twenty minutes, ache was only remotely present, threatening at the edges of the cotton world that swathed me. The mind contained the body, not the other way around.

The medieval Latin word *vagus* means "wandering." *Vagrant, vagabond,* and *vague* share this root. When the vagal nerve was overcome by the synaptic deluge, I was not unconscious, but nor could I be called fully conscious. Mind, like bone, unhinged.

When the clouds wore off, I was a body and a mind, but those two things were distant entities. Only the pain arched, electrically, from one pole to the other, from mental to physical. My bones had betrayed me. They broke their monastic promise of silent and unrecognized existence, the covenant of stability and solid form, and forced the mind—its tenth cranial nerve—to speak as well. It wasn't a question of mind over matter. Mind *was* matter, the only matter, matter experiencing a pain too large for the mind to contain.

This circling begins its next loop: mind, matter, matter, mind, container, contained, or the reverse, and all these years have not been enough to bring understanding. Mind and body loosened in their sockets, stretched too far for an easy, elastic return. Perhaps it was always this way: the vagrant mind, the vagabond bones.

Damage

The Soul-Crushing Science of High-End Bra Shopping

Until 2006, my bra shopping consisted of infrequent trips to the clearance rack at the local department store. I alternated between the same two boring bras, each an identical make and color. Now, on the brink of being hooded as a Doctor of Philosophy, a degree I earned while mothering my first child, I wondered if the time had come to do better by myself. My old reliables were shot, broken strands of elastic curling from the cups. Their beige faux satin had faded to cream with stark white patches under the armpits. I decided that maybe I could scrape some money together and plunk it down on better ones, the kind of bras that were supposed to be sexy and empowering, the kind of bras that my long-suffering husband would not lament.

I will admit that, left to my own devices, this project probably would have died on the vine like so many of my attempts at self-improvement, but I floated the idea to my sister-in-law, wondering abstractly what it would be like to be "fitted" for a bra, and she immediately took charge. I had never shopped at a store that required an appointment, but within weeks of my uttering the words "bra fitting," she'd researched undergarment stores, made the arrangements, and driven from Tennessee to Georgia. With her riding shotgun, I steered my fifteen-year-old Buick LeSabre an hour west of Athens to our allotted fitting time at Phipp's Plaza, the highest of the high-end Atlanta malls.

"Mall" isn't the right word. It's too sullied by food courts and bargain racks. It fails to capture the grandeur we now faced. The parking lot appeared recently vacuumed. I skirted the edge, maneuvering past the valets awaiting the various Escalades and Lexi because only one person parked my Detroit-tastic sofa-on-wheels, and that person was me.

I can't say for sure that uniformed men manicured the hedges along the entry with nail scissors. I can't be certain that the sidewalk was getting one last spit polish before the post-lunch rush. Surely my imagination added the trays of crumpets and finger sandwiches. Even so, if any mall were to offer a free ice sculpture with purchase, this was that mall. Its immense chandelier dripped with crystal. Custom mosaic marble tile floors were set off by polished cherrywood accents. At its center, Olympian columns soared to meet an immaculate oval skylight large enough to accommodate the entry of a reasonably sized zeppelin.

We followed the scent of air-conditioned roses to the bra store, where gentle guitar music and Chanel-suited ladies greeted us, inviting us to survey the stock as we waited for our dressing rooms. We were not to strain ourselves sorting through the merchandise. Our fitting expert was to do any and all work, literally sizing up our boobs for appropriate carriers. We the customers were also to be connoisseurs, appreciating underclothes as art—each bra hung and spotlit as meticulously as any museum *objets*.

My sister-in-law was whisked into one dressing room and I to another. "Room" is the operative word. These were not the pin-scattered stalls of my usual mall. Each generous space had a full-length door with oiled hinges and a heavy knob that clicked shut more securely than the average bank vault. A small ottoman flanked the mirror. I want to say a potted plant sat on a table, but I suspect they would have balked at anything so gauche as a fake fern. This was a store that throve on the sleek austerity of old-money manners mixed with modern sans-serif efficiency.

My consultant asked first to look at my old bra, which I quickly removed and handed to her. She pinched it, her nails a kind of forceps, and sighed. "How many bras do you own?"

"Two for everyday wear and two sports bras," I replied. "I run," I added. These words changed everything. Suddenly she was smiling broadly. Her voice was animated and enthusiastic. "What you really need, then, is a whole bra wardrobe. We recommend a bra for each day of the week, plus two for sleeping and two or three for sports, depending on your activity level."

"I can't do that right now," I said, wanting to be honest with her so that she didn't raise her hopes.

"Of course," she said, whisking my words away like dust under a rug. "What I'd recommend, then, is two new everyday pieces now, which you can alternate, plus one bra for sleeping in and a couple of sports bras. You really need two at the least so that the elastic gets a day off to recover."

Apparently my bra's elastic needed time off like a major league pitcher, an observation I kept to myself.

"What size is this?" Again my consultant lifted the bra, dangling it off a single manicured fingernail.

"It's a 36D," I said.

She pressed her lips together and looked at me sideways as she reached for her tape, casting my old bra to the ottoman and circling my chest with the tape in one swift motion. "As I thought," she said. "You're a 34, not 36. If your bra is loose, your breasts will pull it out of position. I'll be back with some options," she called, bustling away.

Alone, I occupied my half-naked self by looking at an infographic on the wall behind the dressing room door. It showed four women's torsos. In the first, pert tits bounced skyward. These were labeled "healthy." And the next? The next were more . . . familiar. These were gravity bound, the nipples still forward facing but with a notable sag that made them appear more like slightly deflated half-footballs than grapefruit. The infographic's illustration could have been modeled on my own breasts. "Damaged," it read.

The next two pictures showed breasts that sagged into further degrees of distress, culminating in a cartoonish portrait of old-lady boobs that stretched and narrowed to the woman's waistline. I cannot remember the labels on either of these two pictures. My mind was fixated on the word chosen to describe my own.

What did it mean to be damaged? Beyond repair? Short of surgery, there was no going back. More important, back to what? Even in my earliest days, my breasts had never defied gravity like the perky orbs labeled "healthy." I simply wasn't built that way. I had come of age "damaged," my bazoombas beyond hope even from their budding. Time hadn't helped. Breast-feeding, now over, had done no harm, but the stretch marks I'd had since puberty had multiplied. Aside from the added tiger stripes, my breasts were back to pre-pregnancy shape, a shape I'd always accepted as my own, as normal, as genetically dictated. A shape that, the infographic argued, was preventable with the right support. A shape I was now asked to reconceive as damaged.

A quick knock and the brisk opening of the door startled me from these thoughts. "Try this one," my consultant told me—but no sooner had I maneuvered the bra around my waist than she gasped, "No, no. That's *not* how to put on a bra."

This, I must admit, left me baffled. I had approached putting on this bra as I had put on every bra: hooking it behind my back, sliding my arms into the straps, lifting each breast to set it in its cup. In countless locker rooms, I don't remember ever seeing a woman put on a bra any other way.

"If you pull your breasts like that," my consultant said, "it will stretch them out of shape. Here, let me show you. Bend at the waist, like this." She tilted her body, flat-backed, at a forty-five-degree angle from the hips. "You want your breasts to dangle in front of you."

I was fairly certain I had never wanted such a thing, but never mind that; I was still reeling from the idea that years of settling my knockers into my cups had contributed to their damage.

"Now, put your arms through the straps and draw the bra to your chest so that each cup catches its breast. Then, fasten it behind you. Easy."

Gentle reader, there are many times in my life in which I have felt less than coordinated. I found my inner athlete late in life, so I never managed to climb the rope or clear the hurdles in seventh-grade gym. Trying to put on a bra bent at such an angle, though, was more awkward than any feat of athleticism I'd yet tried. The shoulder I had dislocated coming off a horse years earlier refused to bend in the manner required. Looking in the mirror to see where I was going wrong only made matters worse, my hands moving in the opposite direction to the way they needed to go.

"I can help you today," the consultant finally said. "You'll have to practice at home."

She slid me into the bra, situating satin and lace to capture the girls in their optimal position, nipples pointing my way forward through the jungle of life. We repeated this step through several bras.

And honestly, each was beautiful, more carefully constructed than any bra I'd ever worn, but even so, I doubted their functionality. I loved, for instance, the brown check bra with the elastic straps constructed of linked flowers, but would those elasticized daisy chains lie flat under my clothing? And wouldn't the brown show through a white shirt? The demi-cups, too, were lower than I was used to. "Won't I fall out of the top?" I asked.

"We'll try something with more coverage if that will make you more comfortable," she said, her tone peeved, and into the next bra I went. She put me into one bra after another, trying unsuccessfully to mask her increasing irritation as I asked questions.

"What can I have wrapped up for you?" the woman finally asked, as she rehung the last bra.

"I'm really not sure," I said, feeling both dazzled and overwhelmed. I gravitated toward one pale pink bra, which was both functional and comfortable, but still, I had reservations. It didn't seem like me. None of them did.

My consultant sensed my hesitation, and it did not please. She pursed her lips. "I will get a couple sports bras while you make up your mind."

"Actually, I'm pretty happy with the ones I have."

She stared at me for a full second. "The problem with most sports bras," she said, clipping her words now between her whitened teeth, "is that they crush your breasts flat, killing the tissue at the root. Ours don't. I'll be back with two of our most popular models."

It was clear to me now that the woman worked on commission, but I hardly held that against her. I'd worked retail myself, and though my own sales jobs had only paid flat minimum wage, I imagined that she depended on making sales. The need to work was something we shared.

Less clear to me was the "science" being used to support sales. The infographic had been bad enough, but did elastic need rest? Could one actually pull one's breasts out of shape? And since when did breasts have roots? Pondering these mysteries as well as the question of when I had spent this much time topless, I turned over the price tag of one of the bras now piled on the ottoman, the brown check with daisy chain straps.

Now, let's be clear: I had planned to spend some money. I'd figured forty dollars, maybe even fifty per bra if they were really nice. One hundred dollars for two bras was an outlandish sum—I couldn't remember the last time I'd spent so much in a single shopping trip—but I had reconciled myself to the cost because I knew I would wear whatever I bought for years to come. I thought I had prepared myself.

The price tag did not say $40. The tag did not say $50 or even $55. What the tag said was $78.99.

My mind was no longer in the dressing room. My mind was on my bank balance. My mind was on my daughter at home, the next grocery bill, electricity and gas. My mind was on my grad school stipend, a yearly salary of less than $14K a year.

I flipped through the stack. The price tags ran from $110 down to the pink bra, miraculously cheap in comparison at $55. I could see now why I was supposed to choose my favorites before asking their price.

The consultant returned, interrupting my panicked flicking of one tag after another. She turned delicately from my unsightly price-checking and removed the sports bra from its hanger. I bent again at the waist, calculating. How long had this woman spent with me? Twenty minutes? Half an hour? How much would she lose if I didn't make a purchase?

"There." She finished doing the clasps behind me. "How does that compare to the bras you have at home? Better, right?"

I stared at the mirror, my chest smushed into a mono-boob by the tight fabric. Unlike my everyday bras, my sports bras were not cheap. I had selected them after careful research so that I could run with minimal bounceage, and they cost around forty dollars each. My philosophy of beauty is basically that all clothing looks better on a healthy woman. Spending money on sports bras meant not spending money on clothing designed to camouflage and compensate. This bra, to be blunt, was nowhere near as supportive, comfortable, or attractive as the two I had in my drawer at home. "Honestly," I said, "it feels rather snug."

"Of course." Disdain or frustration again pitched her voice high. "It wouldn't be much of a sports bra if it didn't hold you in place."

I've always been a good student, in part because I ask questions when I don't understand a concept, so perhaps that's why I couldn't bite back the next words. "But," I said, "I thought you said that bras that were too tight killed your breasts at the roots?"

She stared at me. Questions were not, apparently, an allowable feature of underclothing commerce. "Would you like to try the other sports bra or not?"

"I really think I'm happy with the ones I have."

"How about sleep bras, then?"

"I'm afraid I'm really not going to sleep in a bra."

"Did you at least decide on any everyday bras?"

I swallowed. "Can I have a moment to think about it?"

She left me then, telling me to let her know if she could be of any further assistance. Frustrated as she was, her southern manners—or at least the formalities of southern manners—held to the end.

I put my old bra back on, trying first to dangle my boobs as instructed before giving up and doing things my usual way. For another twenty minutes I walked around the store with the pink bra's hanger clenched in hand, trying to make up my mind to buy it, before I finally returned it to the rack and went out to sit on the bench near the entry while my sister-in-law finished.

Her consultant drew the lucky straw. My sister-in-law walked away with three new bras that day, all works of art that I'm sure brought her pleasure, but her face fell when I relayed my own experience. "You came here to buy bras," she said, shocked. And truly, I already felt bad enough. I knew I had wasted my consultant's time. My husband, too, would have to deal a little longer with the sad old bit of tortured faux satin. I'd let multiple people, not to mention my own damaged breasts, down.

That's how they get us, isn't it? Working on our guilt, our desire to please others, our aspirations to be all that we can. They tear us down with pseudo-science and infographics. They attack our self-esteem. They damage our self-perception, then promise to rebuild it—for $78.99, or $50, or $199, or whatever price we're willing to pay.

My husband, far from disappointed, laughed with me in the comfort of our kitchen that night, chopping and dicing together as always, because a good sauté makes up for many lacks. Despite my walking away empty handed, our small daughter literally jumped for joy when I walked in our front door, making me feel like the most important person in the world, no matter what my undergarment situation. And what did I find, on the next visit to the clearance rack, but the new version of my tried-and-true Bali underwire, size 34D, $13.95.

Wonder Woman

Here is a picture and a picture and a picture, each magazine-torn as if for collage, but the woman is not making a collage. Look. She fans them in front of you, pointing at each in turn. You can't, this many years removed, summon her words, her voice, her image. You remember only the photographed women in front of you, the beautiful, famous women you could not name, with one exception: Wonder Woman.

She's on your swim towel—not Carter but cartoon. She strides in star-spangled bloomers, red boots, eagled breast. Her cuffs deflect bullets; her tiara cuts; the rope at her waist is a lasso of truth.

You're a strong swimmer, and your fading pool towel proves it, bordered with patch after patch: polliwog, minnow, stingray, sea horse. You're seven, and they're running out of classes to put you in. You have a brown bikini and a blue one, but you prefer the one-piece. You know that the bikinis are cuter, and you'll wear anything your mother gives you if it means you can go to the pool, but the muscle-backed tank suit, sun- and chlorine-bleached, makes you fast and fearless. Even then, these are your priorities.

On the towel, Wonder Woman too wears a one-piece.

The picture woman is a speech therapist. Her room is small as a closet. You sit together in small chairs at a round table. You don't have a lisp or a stutter. You're here because you suck your thumb, and your second-grade teacher has sent you to stop.

In every photo of you at this age, your hair hangs to your nose in a thick mop and springs from pigtails in wild bumps and wayward strands. Your grandfather calls you his Blonde Bombshell. Your grandmother complains that you'll think the world has blonde stripes. She chides your mother, but the hairdresser's scissors can't keep up.

In fact, you see the world clearly, even through the mass of hair. By the time you reach college, you'll call vision your superpower, only half joking. You can read text on computer screens from twenty yards away. It is your party trick: reading at distances. In your forties, the need for reading glasses will come as a blow. Glasses, you know from childhood, are for the alter ego. Glasses are the first thing to toss when you spin into greatness.

In your memory, which may not be trusted, the speech therapist's nails are manicured. Their sharp, polished points rest on each image in turn. She looks at you over the frames of her spectacles. "These women are beautiful—don't you think so?"

Yes.

"See their teeth, how nice and straight they are?" A pointed fingernail stretches to Lynda Carter. "Don't you want nice straight teeth so that you can be beautiful like this?"

Yes.

"If you suck your thumb, your teeth will grow crooked. Do you want that?"

Your desire for beauty is nothing compared to your desire for strength. In five years' time, your teeth will be put in braces. The orthodontist will be surprised to know you were a thumb sucker. Your teeth haven't bucked in spite of predictions. As he works, you stare at the photo of an NFL cheerleading squad, signed with thank-yous on his wall. Their teeth shine like stars.

As a child, you learn you will not be beautiful. You learn other things as well. You learn you can swim and hit a tennis ball. You learn the special place to scratch the ears of dogs and horses to make them lean into your hand. You learn black snakes can be found nesting in sun-warmed cinder blocks. You learn the wonders hidden in the woods behind your house, including the single-plank swing dangling so high from the limb overhead that you can not touch it, no matter how you jump. You learn that, when you play pretend, your friends prefer you to take names like Becky or Brenda and not Mrs. Super Muscle Brainy Brilliant Woman, but you also learn that you can hold that name inside yourself. You learn to lean into the words on pages rather than the images. You learn that you can imagine yourself into other bodies, other worlds. You learn to absorb light with darkness. You learn that bodies are malleable, breakable, miraculous. You learn many wonderous ways a woman may be beauty-filled.

Bread

There is a deep satisfaction to be gained from the feel and smell of the dough as it is kneaded and formed, from that wonderful warm aroma of its baking, and finally from the pride of authorship. The art of bread making can become a consuming hobby, and no matter how often and how many kinds of bread one has made, there always seems to be something new to learn.

—Julia Child, "Breads," in *The Way to Cook*

KNEAD

It started with a simple wish: I wanted to make bread. I know that bread—good fresh bread, already made—is relatively affordable, that Big City Bread is a walkable six blocks away, and that their sesame semolina bâtard perfectly accompanies my partner's homemade tomato basil feta soup, but I wanted to make bread myself. From scratch. From foaming yeast to the satisfying thump that says, "Done." I wanted to make bread, loaves and loaves of it spreading across my counter like a magazine ad. Bread, like my grandmother never made, because with seven children she had too much to do. Bread, like my mother made when I was a child and she was in her natural foods phase: dense, dark loaves scattered with oats. Bread, like my friend's mom made daily back on their dairy farm, where I visited for an August week before my sophomore year of college; the smell coming from her opening oven never left me. No one I know bakes bread anymore. It seems so simple, so satisfying, such a pure, good thing.

I'd argue our culture made a wrong turn when we decided sliced bread was a great thing, the mark by which all subsequent great things would be measured. It is not a great thing. Slicing a whole loaf exposes its inside to air, allowing it to go stale, making preservatives a necessity, and sliced bread robs us of our most communal ritual: breaking bread. With sliced bread, we took the first step from fresh daily loaves to plastic sacks of Wonder. I was beginning to feel the full force of this transgression. Maybe it was my baby, smiling from her highchair, who reminded me, her rattle's shake asking me to put down my books and stop studying for a moment. Maybe it was my struggles to make sure I knew exactly what was going into her little body, to make sure her food was wholesome. Maybe it was the focus on home, the social life that was restricted by feedings and bedtimes. Whatever the cause, I realized that I had allowed simple pleasures, like bread, to sift away like so many grains. Now I wanted them back. Bread was the key. With bread is life. And so I bought some yeast.

> Don't you just love the aroma of fresh-baked bread? It's the smell that says "home."
> —"Yeast Bread Basics," in *Betty Crocker's Cookbook*

RISE

Bread is the physical embodiment of the soul. It symbolizes our highest ambitions and our most basic needs. We can get by on nothing but bread and water, or if we're really desperate, on just "a crust of bread." We can transcend ourselves with a wafer of bread and a sip of wine on a Sunday morning. Bread is the body, and it is more than the body.

Bread rained from the sky in a moment of need.

Bread was on the menu at the Last Supper, and possibly the first.

Bread fed the workers who built Stonehenge and those that erected the pyramids of Egypt.

Jesus ate bread, but so did Pilate. Kings ate white bread while their peasants ate black. Native Americans made bread with flour hand-ground in stone pestles, long before European settlers came to build their flour-grinding waterwheels. Bread is endemic and ubiquitous. It is human. It seems that all cultures have breads in some form or other. The recipe is part of our fabric, creating and sustaining the fabric that creates and sustains it. Reciprocal.

Our word "bread" goes so far back into its Germanic roots that the *OED* lists no predecessors, only near-homophonic variant pronunciations, the Dutch *brood*, the German *Brot*. In Old English, the word "bread" described not only bread itself but any morsel of food. Bread was the minimum essential, an idea at the heart of our slang use of "bread" to mean money—specifically, the amount of money needed to meet pressing bills. Yet bread is also our measure of social class: the upper crust, those who have opulence beyond necessity or even beyond desire.

Bread is both all we need and all we want. Our body, our soul. Rumor declared that Marie Antoinette, callous, said, "Let them eat cake," but man cannot live on cake alone. We are simpler creatures than that. The sugar would kill us. The suggestion that we can live without bread is a capital offense. In eighteenth-century France (a country where they still take their bread eating seriously), they guillotined Marie Antoinette, sliced her, for not recognizing the inalienable right to bread.

> The tradition of baking bread in the home kitchen nearly disappeared in America in the mid-twentieth century—and commercial loaves degenerated, for the most part, into sugar-dosed presliced white bread. Many Americans grew up never having tasted a home-baked, much less whole-grain, loaf.
> —Irma S. Rombauer et al., "Yeast Breads," in *The All New Joy of Cooking*

PUNCH DOWN

I start my loaves early on a Saturday morning, hand-mixing and kneading. By three o'clock I expect to have two French baguettes, shining gold and neatly slashed. I envision them as I knead. Three times, my recipe instructs me, the dough must be punched down and shaped, then given space to re-create itself.

But my bread doesn't make the final rise. I know I didn't kill the yeast—it rose the first two times. I gave the loaves a warm, comfortable environment, my oven, only just heated and then turned off. Yet there is the dough, undeniably unrisen. Inexplicably, a flop.

I'm irritated right down to my hands. The very joints accuse me: I made them do all that work, knead that punched-down dough, stretch and roll the resistant mound into raw loaves, and for what? I'm an amateur, and somewhere along the line I made an amateur mistake. A morning of my life gone that I won't get back again, and nothing to show for it. Now I'll have to read twice as fast if I hope to finish Charlotte Smith's long novel for class, and I am a slow, slow reader. I knew I would have this work to do, but the bread was supposed to make up for it. Instead I'm breaking small, hard loaves into bits to toss on the grass.

I am faced with nasty facts: (1) My search for simplicity has made my life more hectic. (2) Even my insatiable squirrels won't eat this loaf. It sits, sniffed but uneaten, on the lawn.

My partner is laughing at me, trying to make me laugh with him as he laughs at me. "Let's walk over to Big City," he says. "We can get *good* bread to go with dinner." My knuckles, which have been punching down dough all morning, have an urge to punch again.

I wanted to make it myself. I wanted authorship over my bread, like Julia said. I feel as obstinate as a child. I am very close to a temper tantrum.

> You've let the dough over-rise, and it has fermented. Don't throw it out. You can still make beautiful bread because the fermented dough will act like an old-fashioned "levain," or starter. . . . You'll probably produce a bread with much more character and texture than usual.
> —Julia Child, "Don't Murder the Yeast and Other Random Notes," in *The Way to Cook*

RISE

My bread did not rise. What kind of soul is that? It failed me, and my squirrels. It took days of rain to finally soak it to crumbs and carry it into the earth, the bread and water that sustained no one.

Maybe bread is not at the root of all things. I looked under P in the dictionary, scanning etymologies, trying to find the French for bread, *pain*, at the roots of words. Perhaps in "penance" or "pancreas," sweetbreads. *Pain in the ass.* I can't find it.

Still, there is something in me that yearns: I want the steam that comes from a broken loaf. The aroma of it will fill the house and lift me, my soul if not my body. I will transcend, if only for a moment, my modern life. My own hands will be the ones to break the bread, open it, expose its steaming warm center. My deadlines will not be on my mind. The baby will smile, knowing that this is a good thing, as good as it gets.

Building Tall

I measured the garage in Megans, an inchworm kind of measuring. I figured it would take three little sisters to be building tall. "Yeah, you can do it," I said. "It's safe."

"You sure?" She squinted at me, small and brown in the sun. She was four and I was six. I would know.

"Definitely."

I looked back at the garage, thought about how tall it looked, and added, "Use the umbrella, though. Like a parachute."

She hesitated only a moment. Our friend Kim stared wide-eyed at the roof, pale under her freckles. Megan turned and flew over the gravel and up the steps in her orthopedic shoes. She disappeared and reappeared, on the roof, smiling.

I don't know why I was so sure, but I believed her flight was possible, though I would have not jumped myself. My sister was always braver than me, always able to do impossible things.

She popped open her red umbrella, its little plastic knobs scraping against skin striped pale by leg braces. Kim said, "I can't watch, I can't watch," but her eyes would not turn away.

I thought Megan would float to the ground like Mary Poppins, but she fell fast. The umbrella inside-outed itself against its metal spines. Yet, when her shoes hit the ground, they sounded like triumph, and she raced to the rooftop to jump again.

The Only Girl in the Known Universe

When I was four years old, George Lucas offered me an unlikely gift. I was at an Ohio drive-in, nestled snugly in our mid-seventies Dodge Ramcharger, with my mother, father, sister, and Uncle Bob, when Lucas opened my palm and placed something warm inside, something impossibly small and so white that it appeared to glow like the pinprick stars beyond the giant screen. "This is power," he said. "I call her Leia."

I don't remember much else about seeing *Star Wars* that first night. I have long lost count of the number of times I've seen it since. For me as for most other children of the seventies, the movie was an ever-presence. We argued over whether Han or Luke was the good guy, just like we argued over whether Kit or the General Lee was a better car. Every Halloween, our stores filled with plastic sack costumes and masks with every character's face. We tilted chairs over to be the cabins of our X-Wings, ptchu-ing out laser beams to take down the legions of tie fighters that filled our living rooms.

From the moment Princess Leia appeared onscreen, my friends and I loved every inch of her, from her flowing dress to her elaborate side buns. We wanted to inhabit her skin, to take on her confidence and resolve. We knew immediately Leia was no ordinary princess, no demure damsel-in-distress. Surrounded by danger on every side, she antagonized her captors with a fierce and unflinching wit: "Governor Tarkin, I should have expected to find you holding Vader's leash. I recognized your foul stench when I was brought on board." *Yes*, we cheered. *Tell him! Stick it to the man.*

Luke and Han may have freed her from her cell, but following the men only led her into greater danger. Leia knew this before they did and mocked their lack of foresight even as the chase was on: "Some rescue! You came in here, but didn't you have a plan for getting out?" She forged the path that would lead them from danger, jumping into a garbage chute without a moment's girly hesitation or squeamishness. Years later my proper British aunt, walking in as this scene played on our VCR, witnessed Leia blast the pursuing Storm Troopers to create their escape. "Well done, madam!" my aunt said, her Queen's English ringing with well-earned awe. Well done indeed. The scene was a dramatic departure from the women we had seen or would see in so many movies. Leia was my first glimpse at a female badass.

As a child, I didn't own a single *Star Wars* action figure, but my neighbor Tommy had them all, from Walrus Man to Hammerhead, from the Millennium Falcon to the X-Wing Fighter. Going to his house to play, my sister and I would begin each game the same way, fighting over who got to be Leia. My mother, sensible and sick of our arguing, suggested we could both be Leia. After all, Tommy had multiple Leias in every outfit. Why not pretend there were two women characters, give one another name?

We merely rolled our eyes. Tommy had his pick of characters, male action figures lying around him, good and evil, but there was only one Leia.

How strange that it was only as an aging Carrie Fisher underwent round after round of body critique that this would fully dawn on me: Leia wasn't the only female action figure. In those first films, Leia was the only girl.

Check it out:

Major male characters from *Star Wars* episodes 4–6	Major female characters from *Star Wars* episodes 4–6
Han	Leia
Luke	
Darth Vader	
Chewbacca	
Lando Calrissian	
Jabba the Hut	
C3PO	
R2D2	
Emperor Palpatine	
Yoda	
Obi-Wan Kenobi	
Boba Fett	

Some might argue that the droids are non-gendered, but both are given male pronouns ("That R2 unit is in fine condition. I've worked with him before") and C3PO has a male speaking voice.

And things don't get much better if we include the minor characters. Yes, we have Aunt Beru and that one girl dancer who gets fed to the aptly named rancor in Jabba's pit, but both are killed almost as soon as they enter the film. Admiral Ackbar is male, as is his fleet of X-Wing pilots, every last Sandperson or Jawa, and the entire Empirical Army. The emperor, his generals, and even the lowliest Storm Trooper? Men, men, men. Leia is the one woman of any significance in the entire dick-swinging universe.

This fact is so achingly obvious that it should have been clear to me even at four years old, but it only strikes me now. "Strikes" being the appropriate verb: the fact woke me up one night like a fish slap to the face. How could I be so blind? How could I miss so obvious a fact?

I suspect I know: In 1978, having even one woman with a degree of agency was a step forward. And really, things haven't changed much in the *Star Wars* universe in the intervening years. Even in the more recent *Star Wars* movie *The Force Awakens*, a quick glance at IMDb shows that men outnumber women nearly three to one, yet it is being lauded as one of the most progressive casts for racial and gender equity. Our standards are that off-kilter.

What is all the more troubling to me is the evolution Leia's character takes over the course of the first three films. Ask any *Star Wars* fan about the mistakes in *Return of the Jedi*, and they are likely to focus on the lame death of Boba Fett or the cloyingly precious Ewoks. To both these complaints I say, yes, fine, but they pale in comparison to the mistake of the metal bikini, the outfit that turned a rebel leader into the object of sexual fantasies faster than Greedo could fire a blaster.

The bikini was in the film for mere minutes, but as soon as it appeared, it forever changed the perception of Leia from rebel to concubine. Wikipedia has a full page devoted to the outfit, an honor not matched by any of her other looks. Leia's Victorianly chaste dress in *A New Hope* was virginal white from turtleneck to booted toe. Unlike so many of today's female superheroes, Leia did not gain her power from her sexual manipulation. In that first film she didn't flirt to get her way. Faced with the sexiest space pirate this side of the Degoba System, she dismissed him as a scruffy-looking nerf herder. In that first 1977 film and its 1980 sequel, Leia was her own woman.

Unfortunately, as soon as Leia appeared in the bikini, all of this was moot. It didn't matter that she would choke her captor with her own chain (what a metaphor!). It didn't matter than she would continue the movie in sensible pants-and-poncho forestwear. It didn't matter that she would outrun and outmaneuver Imperials on their speeder bikes. Walking away from the film, what stuck in the minds of so many viewers was a new sexualized Leia. The bikini had forcibly over-inscribed every other view.

An informal sampling of Facebook friends responding to my question "Quick poll: what are your feelings on Leia's brown bikini in JEDI?" resulted in a telling if unsurprising gender divide. My male friends tended to look back on the bikini fondly. One confessed, "To this day I have a base, carnal response to even thinking of it—let alone SEEING it. I first saw it when I was 15 years old so that probably has something to do with it." Another wrote, "Let's just say it helped shape one of the better parts of every ComicCon."

My female friends were more divided. Those not bothered by the outfit generally pointed out that, even bikini-clad, Leia took out Jabba, thus showing that she was still the same woman no matter what the garb. One went farther, saying, "I thought it was perfect—very sex bondage, making Jabba all the more repulsive." Yet I can't help but wonder if it isn't symptomatic of a social sickness that the underlying assumption here is that sexual exploitation is worse if done by someone who looks "repulsive" than it would be if the dominating power were an attractive man. (*Fifty Shades of Grey*, anyone?)

Of my female friends who objected to the bikini, the varying nature of the objections was, in itself, instructive. "It was unnecessary and went against her character," wrote one. "Plus, Luke's plan was ridiculous in the first place." Another (male) friend challenged her, writing, "I don't think being silent in those circumstances was demonstrative of weakness, nor against her character. She was chained to a 2-ton blob who could have yanked her head off of her body. Her strength was in biding her time instead of displaying her usual irreverent and reckless behavior which would have certainly cost her her life." To which my female friend replied, "I don't think she would have gone along with the plan in the first place, and I see her involvement in the plan as nothing more than a way to get Fisher into a sexy outfit for the viewers."

As my male friend points out, the scene endorses self-silencing as a strategy necessary for protection, and though he sees this as a part of her character, her belligerence when captured in *A New Hope* suggests otherwise. In the third film, Leia doesn't question Luke's plans as she did in *A New Hope*. Her willingness to challenge her captors in previous movies did not result in harm, but though Han mouths off to Jabba, Leia won't. Her character here *has* changed. The smart and sassy Leia has been overwritten by quietude. The rules in this movie are different for Leia, more traditional, more limiting. "Don't talk," the Jabba scene says to women everywhere. "Your voice will not help you here. Your voice is one we never really cared for anyway."

For me as for many female audience members, the sexuality and power dynamics of the bikini, like the lack of women in general, would not register until much, much later. "It's funny," one female Facebook friend wrote, "but I actually didn't realize how sexual it was until I was in my 20s and on *Friends* Rachel got dressed up as Leia for Ross. Then I finally realized, 'Oh!!!'" I nodded as I read her post. My own experience was similar. As a child, I didn't know what to think of the outfit other than to be dimly aware that it wasn't meant for me. White-dress Leia might have been, but this new Leia was designed to serve another audience.

The ultimate crime of the metal bikini is that it turned Leia from a force of personality into merely a body. It situated Leia in the old binary: she'd been a virgin; she was now a whore. The Leia who walked into Jabba's lair as a voice- and gender-disguised bounty hunter armed with a thermal detonator could command a room. The Leia who leaves is something altogether different. From the moment she appears in the bikini, the outfit overwrites the Leia that was and the Leias that will be, a fact that has only now become apparent. When seeing her in *The Force Awakens* where she wears a kind of hybrid version of her Hoth and Endor battle clothes, the viewers who once were excited by the sexual bondage/bikini fantasy are now proportionately repulsed, resulting in a backlash documented in the

Washington Post article "Carrie Fisher to Haters: Youth and Beauty Are Not Accomplishments." The sexualized body is not allowed to age. In the minds of so many fans, sex slave Leia cannot become General Leia. She may have escaped Jabba, but she can't escape the image of her own exposed and captive body.

In the wake of the 2015 movie and the numerous articles it sparked, I found myself wrestling with a number of questions: Would we see her rank of general as the natural outcome of a series of promotions for the girl who stood up to Tarkin and Vader if that girl hadn't been silenced in subsequent movies? Would audiences have accepted an aging Leia better if we'd seen more of her in action, fulfilling her Jedi promise? Why didn't the screenwriters see Leia, who once retrieved top secret plans and smuggled them under the nose of the whole galactic Empire, as capable enough to act on her own to retrieve her son rather than waiting on her wayward and anything-but-reliable husband? How many of the writers of *The Force Awakens* grew up fantasizing about a bikini-clad Leia? How many forgot what she stood for?

Ultimately, I don't know whether any of this is Lucas's fault. As a writer myself, I know how difficult it is to predict how an audience will interpret an image and what they will carry away. Perhaps we were supposed to remember her triumph over the gigantic flaccid penis on his throne. Perhaps it's not Lucas's fault that the image that burned itself into audience members' minds was only the bound and silenced girl.

But why *was* Leia the only woman? And why was it necessary that she be stripped at all? Lucas gave me Leia at a time when I was a child, when the idea of a powerful woman acting of her own volition could shape the way I saw my own capabilities. Far more than Luke, Leia represented a new hope for girls across the country. But the Empire, as always, struck back.

The World Within, the World Without

A Thought List

There are parts of the self that are undeniable. Writing and riding: I've tried quitting them both. I've failed.

The last few years have introduced me to the panic attack. I was given cause: *Salon* published an article called "It's the End of the World and We Know It." An increasing number of scientists believe that the human race won't last another hundred years. More recently, a commentator revised that estimate, saying that, if we continue as we are, the world will be uninhabitable in twenty-five years. I remind myself that no one really knows the future, but here it is, written, feeling like fact. I have children. I love them. The joy they bring me is immeasurable. Ask, and I'll say I want every happiness for them. They have been and are my own truest source of happiness. Yet at this moment, I don't want my children to have children, no matter what joy they may bring. I don't want them to know this ache, this helplessness. I don't want them to lie awake, as I do, stricken with the panic that our world will become too damaged for joy.

Homophonics: If you ride and write, people will often think you are speaking of one when you're speaking of the other. There is a truth that lives in the heart of this confusion.

Writing hurts when I write true. I would rather not think about painful things or see in each sentence my failure to capture the full truth of them, and so at twenty-five I took a job in fund raising for the U.S. Equestrian Team. I wrote letters asking rich people for money, a kind of writing that required no depth and, therefore, no yearning ache to do better. I didn't have to write poetry or fiction or essays ever again. Yet, in the quiet of lonely evenings, I found myself writing a manual. I thought I was writing a how-to for beginning riders: how to select a horse, how to put your foot in a stirrup and lift yourself into the saddle, how to communicate with body weight and pressure. Only later would I realize I was writing for myself. The book was not a manifesto because I didn't know then what manifestos were. I couldn't acknowledge that I was a writer even though I couldn't stop writing. Before the year ended, I enrolled in grad school to study creative writing. I left my job. I wrote back into pain and paid tuition for the opportunity. I didn't make many right choices in my twenties, but that was one.

Joy: a temporary insanity culminating in elation.

Riding a horse is the language of one body talking to another body. Riding is a language in which words are irrelevant.

I've been thinking a lot about the purpose of life, the time allotted, and the best way to spend it. I've heard the sundial adage: "Every hour wounds. The last one kills." I don't believe the first part. The second is undeniable.

That *Salon* article? I am aware of its contradictions, how the threat of plague/pandemic actually mitigates the threat of climate change and famine, both of which are fueled by overpopulation. The horsemen gallop in opposing directions. We can't know where they'll carry us. None of this makes me feel better.

Two off-track Thoroughbreds have run away with me. One fall cracked my helmet and knocked me senseless, the other dislocated my shoulder. After the first, I decided I would stop riding horses. After the second, I knew myself better. Sometimes pain is not the problem. Sometimes there are horses you can't control. Neither of these facts will stop fear from pooling in your chest as the horse's legs stretch into a bolt.

Art asks the artist to honestly represent an aspect of the world. *Why* we should is less clear.

I'd like to believe that humanity can pull out of this headlong rush and save ourselves. The trees are leafing out against the blue sky and it seems hopeful enough until I allow myself to know that it may not last. Or rather, that the sky will last but we won't.

Rethink "communicate." Take it to its root: *communis*, common, shared. Commune, communion: the sharing of a sentiment, a feeling, an emotion. Joy, doubt, fear.

I fear climate change more than pandemic in the same way I fear cancer more than heart attack.

Writing fiction is an act of self-erasure. I strive to write characters so distinct that they don't necessarily think or act or talk like me, their writer. This is a feat of creative empathy that's nearly impossible to achieve. I try, knowing that I will fail. Empathy is a muscle I would like to exercise. Even now. Even with people whose heads I don't want to occupy: racists, gun enthusiasts, climate change deniers, Trumpeters. Story digs a tunnel into the dark. I feel for these characters, taking their sentiments temporarily as my own. Delving, what I unearth again and again is fear.

"Throw your heart over the fence and the horse will follow."

I want to manifest emotion through the page, to communicate it into another body. This must be done with care and an eye toward ethics. Narrative is a magic easily used for harm. *See* politics.

"Too damaged for joy," I wrote. How mawkish. How maudlin. I have indulged my panic on the page. I would tear those sentences out, if only they weren't honest. I want to be straight with you. I must acknowledge fear and feel its heavy muscle pulling me one way and another if I have any hope of mastering it.

When our so-called president exited the Paris Accord, all I could feel was rage.

Unscrew yourself at the waist. Attach new, more powerful legs. Riding is the language of a mind talking to a mind through the media of muscle and skin. Riding is a melding of one body to another. Thought translates to movement. Each muscle must be independent and precise. Doubt, and it moves the horse. Panic, and it moves the horse. Dressage means training, and training means mental and physical control. Control means regulating your behavior and movement. Control means check—originally, a check of accounts, one register or "roll" against another, then evolving as a check on one's behavior.

Writing and riding, the empathetic arts. I know fear. I know how easy it is to communicate its disease.

On the back of a horse, the sky is bluer. On the back of a horse, the air is fresher, spiced with the scent of sweat and broken grass. On the back of a horse, there is always a breeze. On the back of a horse, it is impossible not to be in love with the world. On the back of a horse, there is no future and no past because there is no moment besides this one.

Fear: I don't know how to move the world. Science shows that the carbon level is our fault and suggests we might be able to fix it, if only we would. The "we" is billions. I don't have a fulcrum or a lever long enough. No one person does.

Dance is the art of the body, of control, of the moment and the movement, the art of developing muscle, of extension and collection. Somewhere in that sentence I started to talk about riding.

An abundance of humanity is destroying our planet. An abundance of humanity might fix it. Can we allow that hope? I want to move you.

"Grant me the serenity to accept the things I cannot change, / Courage to change the things I can, / And wisdom to know the difference."

I have today, and today is beautiful. I share it with my children. "Loveliest of trees, the cherry now," I whisper.

Any little tension affects a ride. I carry mine in elbows and shoulders, and I must imagine elastic in its place. A trainer once said, a horse can no more move with a tight rider on its back than a gymnast can perform in tight blue jeans. If panicked, the rider loses the ability to communicate anything other than fear. The horse hears that fear and raises with its own. It becomes a rigid, racing thing, dangerous to itself and its rider.

"The only thing we have to fear is fear itself." When FDR spoke those words, the warring world offered a hell of a lot to fear. That doesn't mean he wasn't right.

How exactly do you throw your heart?

I once aspired to write words that would outlive me, art built for posterity. I didn't know if I could do it, but the knowing didn't matter. What mattered was the attempt. But what if there is no posterity to write for?

I desperately want that last sentence to appear paranoid when I read this back to myself in twenty years' time. I would be happy to look foolish if only it meant I was wrong.

I'm awake again. It's three in the morning. I can hear my son's breath across the hall. A hand is again inside my chest, a fist in my ribs where my heart should live. Yesterday I read that some seventeen-year cicadas emerged four years early. "Climate change" whispered on every wing. The words echoing in my brain: it may be too late to reverse.

The wisdom to know the difference. The wisdom to know the difference. The wisdom to know the difference.

The fist gripping my heart—can it pitch?

Fear is a headlong horse. We need all our strength to curb it, but horses always were stronger than their riders. Something beyond strength allows direction. Something beyond direction allows partnership. Something beyond partnership allows love. If there is any hope, we must make it our bridle. And if there is no hope?

Terror is unsustainable. I can't stay here, even though I keep visiting. I need to translate panic into action, make feeling into movement. No one knows what the future holds.

"No one ever came to grief except honourable grief through riding horses. No hour of life is lost that is spent in the saddle. Young men have often been ruined through owning horses, or through backing horses, but never through riding them, unless of course they break their necks, which, taken at a gallop, is a very good death to die." Winston Churchill, from his memoir *My Early Years*

Phrasing is a musical thing, a measured movement, a cadence. Each sentence has a gait with beats that move it. I bend them in my mind, feel the stride as they hit the straightaway. I delight in their jump, their power for flight.

Fear can catapult or cripple. Used wisely, it can impel. Harness fear and it can be put to work. I must check and steer it into a slower, more purposeful gallop.

At sixteen, I thought I'd never ride again. At nineteen, I put my feet in the irons. Panic seized every muscle, but so did love. This horse could plant me. This horse could break me. It had happened before. Yet if this were to be how I go, it would be a good death to die. The horse and I breathed in snorts, our hearts moving blood and air through different bodies of muscle. We borrowed courage from one another, our minds growing closer until thought translated through skin.

It was said that Generation X were the first generation destined to be financially less well off than our parents, a prediction that came true for me but that strikes me now as too banal for words. How can I worry about financial well-being at a time like this?

hoofbeats hoofbeats hoofbeats

Snowpocalypse in Georgia, nearly a decade ago: The untempered pine boughs creaked under the strange weight of snow. I watched as they swayed above my children making their first snowman. Any tree could fall, crushing them. Trees had fallen and would continue to fall throughout the neighborhood all that day. I watched, working through a familiar calculation, the weighing of danger against adventure. They must be allowed to love this world as I have been. I want their lives to be rich and full, which sometimes means giving up safety. I know this from riding horses, a dangerous sport: joy involves risk.

I have no patience for willful ignorance. Pretending the world isn't broken does not allow us to fix it. I'm awoken at three a.m. by some yahoo in a truck with the world's loudest exhaust as he peels down one road after another. Already I'm chastising myself: I don't like to see the world in yahoos. It's not a helpful stance. He is so goddamned afraid that he roars us awake in the depth of night, yet his barbaric yawp will have as limited an effect as all my attempts to limit the damage I cause by existing.

Acceptance, courage, wisdom: What can I change? I wash plastic bags, walk to work, combine errands into single trips, avoid airplane travel, add insulation to the attic, turn down the thermostat in winter and turn it up in summer. I do what I can, knowing it isn't enough.

I tell myself to put my faith in science to guide us toward answers just as I put my faith in art to steer the feelings that guide our actions. I can only trust this moment. When I step tentatively to the future, test my weight against its flimsy, fragile boards, they offer no promises or security.

A writer must learn to trust her obsessions.

I take my son and daughter to the park. We toss a baseball and words between us in the evening light. We share smiles. I want the world for them.

Scones

A Recipe

Your British father tells you that traditional scones are made with currants, and the recipes you look up one after another agree, but you'll dismiss this idea because you're American, and though tradition may have gotten you as far as scones, it didn't get you as far as currants. Opt instead for lemon-ginger in honor of his mother, your Gran. Crystallized, ginger was her favorite, and your mother bought it for her, dipped in dark chocolate, year after year after year on Christmas, which is tradition enough.

Dig in the back of the top shelf for the crystallized ginger. Decide how spicy you're feeling. Six-pieces-level spicy? Seven? Chop ten pieces, pulling eight nice-sized chunks to the side for later.

In a bowl: 1¾ cups flour, 3 tablespoons sugar, 2½ teaspoons baking powder, ½ teaspoon salt. Salt is not optional. Stir with a whisk that's probably too small for the job but is the only whisk you own, one you bought in a grocery store years ago. Tell your son that it won't be too much longer, even though you've only just begun.

Take a stick of butter and cut off two-thirds. Put the remaining bit on the butter tray. Slice the two-thirds hunk lengthwise into four slabs, then turn them on their long axis and slice them lengthwise in four again. Slice these bars crosswise, letting each cut fall apart into neat sixteenths that make you feel like a math genius and cooking pro. Relish this. Should the scones fail, you'll still have this victory.

At this point, every recipe will suggest you cut the butter in to keep it cold, but the butter always gets stuck in the pastry cutter and you have to pull it free with your fingers, which warms the fat anyway and is a pain and makes another utensil to clean. Forgo the cutter. Enjoy how cool the flour is on your fingers, how fine, how soft, as you press the butter in.

Let your mind wander as you sift and press the flour and butter in your fingertips. Remember the girl who told you that it doesn't count as being the daughter of an immigrant if your immigrant father was only British. Know all the ways she was right and know all the ways she was wrong. Remember the precision of your grandmother's back garden with its perfect border of perfect flowers. Wonder why you even own that stupid pastry cutter.

Every scone recipe worth its salt will now suggest you chill the dough for an hour, but the clock is ticking toward ten, and these are supposed to be breakfast. Your son is circling the kitchen like a shark sniffing blood. Skip this step.

Retrieve the flour-silted whisk and a glass measuring cup. In it, beat an egg with maybe a third of a cup of the last bit of half-and-half your husband had bought for his coffee.

Zest a lemon into the flour and toss it with a fork. Pour in the eggy half-and-half, adding milk from the carton if it looks too dry. Pour a glass for your son while you're at it. Tell him *nearly*.

Add the ginger when everything is almost coming together. Check to make sure your oven is on. It isn't. Turn it to 400°.

Roll the dough with the rolling pin you found at an old Idaho farmer's estate sale, its wood still rich and oiled with butter from a hundred pies and biscuits made by a woman you never knew. You want it thick and not too pretty. Make it round. Round-ish. Nearly round-ish with rough sides patted in. Call these lacy. Roughness as décor, the personal touch.

Juice the lemon into the quick-rinsed measuring cup. Brush the juice over the dough. Sprinkle liberally with raw sugar. Cut the dough circle in half and in half and in half and in half. Press one reserved ginger chunk into the middle of each of the eight parts.

Bake ten minutes, twelve—until the edges toast. Wash the dishes while they bake. Remember your British aunt, a caterer, how quick she was with the washing up. Think of her frenetic scrubbing and the way it shook her perfectly coiffed hair free, if only temporarily. Remember how her skirts only loosely matched her thin sweaters, a British version of matching. Remember how even her slippers had heels. You inherited none of her formality. In fact, you can't think of a single trait you share except perhaps the ability to get every dish cleaned, dried, and put away before the timer beeps.

Set the scones on a rack. Your family is with you now, the living and the departed, summoned by the scent. Notice the remaining half a pot of coffee, still hot on the warmer. Make a cup of tea instead, Yorkshire Gold, with sugar and milk. The scones are hot, crisp on the surface but soft and steaming inside. Their butterfat feeds something deep. Sip your tea. You were born in Ohio and raised in the West, but this morning, remember you're only American-ish.

My First Name

This new doctor smiles as he enters the room, as if we're sharing a joke although we've never met before. "Tell me," he says, "how many people get your name right on the first try?"

I struggle to remember whether it's ever happened. Maybe once? Even then, it's possible they got an inside tip from a helpful someone who happened to know me. "It's Welsh," I say, answering the question he'll ask next, as if this explains.

You don't meet too many Siâns, though my name is not as uncommon as people assume. It's usually in books of baby names. If you look for me on social media, you'll have to choose which Siân Griffiths you mean. Google my name, and you'll find a professor of public health, a mezzo soprano, a landscape architect, the education editor of the *Sunday Times*, and a bunch of other not-mes. U2's The Edge named his daughter Siân, and we share our name with the actresses Siân Phillips (*Dune*; *I, Claudius*; *Clash of the Titans*), Siân Clifford (*Fleabag*), and Siân Brooke (*Sherlock*). This isn't to say that Siân is a common name—it's never broken the top thousand names in the Social Security list—but we do put up a respectable showing, with somewhere between five and thirty-five Siâns named in the United States each year.

I wonder if my mother guessed, when she chose my name, that she was putting me in a group, making me one of the Siâns as other people might be Karens or Brads. Perhaps all names do this, creating a bond between people simply because they share a word, and my name only makes me more aware of it.

None of this information would help my doctor or answer his question, because the answer I'm giving him, the correct pronunciation of my name, is technically wrong.

The writer L. M. Montgomery, whose own Anne-with-an-e insisted on the relationship between her word and her person, wrote that, if a rose were called a thistle or a skunk cabbage, it simply could not smell as sweet. In grad school, my cohort spent the summer translating French literary phrases into English to fulfill our language requirement, including "A rose, if you called it anything else, it would still smell the same way." The translation made me newly aware of the alchemy inherent in language. Surely, we thought, Shakespeare himself would have to agree that somehow, wrapped up in the cadence of sound and spelling, we create an element of the thing itself.

There was a time when I didn't love having to correct pronunciations. To be honest, there are still times when I avoid giving my name to strangers—baristas, the Costco pizza pickup—because I know they'll ask me to repeat it or will write down some ludicrous version. As I have corrected people on how to pronounce my name, I in turn have been corrected by the actual Welsh, who are none too pleased with my mother's version, a variant negotiated with my father. Even so, there's also something about this experience that I recognize as formative. All my life, I have had to insist upon my own identity.

My mother was a Marie, as was her mother. The oldest of her six younger brothers is a Francis, like his son and our grandfather. My uncle Frank is a Francis Joseph and my Uncle Joe is a Joseph Francis. My mother's side of the family is big on name recycling, with names shared by parents and children and uncles and cousins. It's a way of paying homage and creating unity. Or, if you see things like my mother, it's a failure of creativity.

In the months leading up to my birth, my mom wrestled with these points of view. She wanted something fresh, but she also wanted the name to tie to my family history, her own and my father's. He was British with roots in Wales, and if you want to give your child a name that is neither overrepresented nor invented outright, Welsh names are a good option. Hence, Siân.

There were two problems: (1) the recent appearance and naming of my cousin Sean, which would have made me a near homophone, a repeat, and (2) my mother's difficulty pronouncing the Welsh in her thick Philadelphia accent. And so I'm a Siân who's pronounced as a Shane. Because my mother wanted to be different. Because my mother loved cowboys and adventure. Because these same loves would draw her west, to California and Idaho, where I grew up. She settled on the pronunciation before she settled on the spelling, and so I have a two-page birth certificate. The original lists me as Shane Griffiths, my first first name. The second, created the next day, is a name correction changing the spelling to Siân.

Kids in elementary school told me that Siân was a boy's name, and even though they were wrong, perhaps this allowed me to think myself unbound by the conventions of gender. They called me Siân the Pain, a literally childish attempt to weaponize the sound of myself against me, and the hurt it caused created something too, something difficult to articulate but bound to sound and language and poetry. Years later, I still wonder if pain is a part of my writing—a trope, a motivation, a rhythm. Like Anne, I have to believe that words create, in part, the thing they identify. A Siân, if you called it anything else, would be an altered thing. A Siân, by any other name, would not be a Siân.

Writing *Boudica*

I spent much of 2016 drafting a screenplay for a movie that will never be made.

Let's say, *probably* never. It's less depressing, and the project has always needed a dash of foolish hope. *Probably* is the word that started me going, though I knew the length of the odds, and *probably* is the word that keeps me tinkering with it even now, reconceiving the plot and conflict. *Probably* allows me to stay obsessed. I have faith in *probably*, because *probably* has created the space in which my entire career has come to exist, elbowing its way outward until "writer" became a part of my identity. Writing a screenplay would be no different.

And yet I wasn't ignorant. I knew the common wisdom, which said that the first step in selling a screenplay is to move to Los Angeles.[1] I knew and know myself as well. I am not going to give up my home or profession. I don't have the people skills necessary to pitch or to hobnob, both traits necessary for a career in Hollywood. Besides, I didn't want to write screenplays. I wanted to write *a* screenplay.

The idea had been percolating since sometime in the late 1990s when I first played Sid Meier's *Civilization II*. I have never been much of a gamer, but when my college boyfriend brought home a sale-discounted copy, I was pulled in. The premise was simple: you chose a famous historical leader and built a culture, erecting cities and monuments and pursuing technological and scientific advancements, all in the hope of beating the other computer-played cultures to colonize space. I'd played a bootleg

---

1   This has been less true during the coronavirus pandemic, but only time will tell whether the ironic flexibility of living location afforded by lockdown will remain true.

copy of the original, but the new version fleshed out the world. More important, it included additional female leaders on the list of those you could play, including one I had never heard of: Boadicea.

Curious, I looked her up. I may even have googled her on that new search engine, but more likely I searched Yahoo or Excite. I found a few different spellings of her name (Boadicea, Boudicca, Boudica) and a spotty but compelling story. The sites told of a Celtic "warrior queen" who led her people on the most successful British revolt ever launched against the Roman Empire, driving the colonizers from the land of the Iceni (now Norfolk) to Londinium (London) in a series of brutal victories. Before the revolt, she and her husband Prasutagus, a local chieftain, had lived peaceably with their colonizers. In return the Romans had allowed Prasutagus to maintain his kingdom and guaranteed it to his heirs, who would rule in conjunction with Rome. Yet when he died, the Romans reneged on their bargain, seizing total control and plundering the kingdom. Boudica protested, but rather than acquiescing, the Romans flogged the grieving widow and raped her daughters, sparking a ferocious maternal outrage that would manifest in war.

I could see it all unspooling on film: part *Gladiator*, part *Braveheart*, but woman-centered. I saw Boudica standing on a cliff's edge, the coastal wind whipping her red hair, the bucolic British countryside spanning out behind her, dotted with round thatch-roofed houses. I saw a spear clutched in her hand, her wool cloak fluttering, the Celtic knot of her brooch. I read the tragic nobility of her expression and the determination to win her country back against rapists and cheats, against colonizers, against an all-male Roman army. Sure, she lost in the end, but so did William Wallace. So did Rocky. So did virtually every hero from a Shakespearean tragedy. Defeat isn't a problem so long as the writer lays in an alternate victory to be read in its ashes.

For years, I wanted someone to write her movie so that I could go see it. Sometime during grad school, I began to wonder if by "someone" I meant me. I imagined a blockbuster, but one unlike any blockbuster I'd ever seen. This would be a movie about female power. More than a decade before *Wonder Woman* made the vision a reality, I saw ass-kicking women fighting alongside men. Better still, this story was not some Marvel or DC fantasy. Boudica's story was true.

Or, at least, the bones of the story were true. The thin history left ample room for invention. Perhaps too much. Only two ancient writers, Publius Cornelius Tacitus and Cassius Dio, captured Boudica's story. Both were Romans, both writing decades and a continent removed from the woman herself. Their histories are creative and contradictory and deeply biased. Roman historians are famous for inflating the odds against their countrymen, stoking the sense of Rome's military greatness. As contemporary historians Richard Hingley and Christina Unwin point out, "Tacitus used events in Britain to moralise about the state of the empire in more general terms" and "Dio's account of Boudica has been characterized as 'inventions and inversions' of Tacitus's writings." They wrote with agendas that were truer polestars than fact.

I was indebted to Tacitus and Dio for capturing Boudica's story, but I worried over the paucity of information as well as its unreliability. Though later scholars would try to fill in the gaps, there remained an abundance of unknowns. In all the histories, Boudica's daughters have no names. I didn't know her age or theirs. The references name her husband, but they disagree about his relationship with the Roman colonizers. In some accounts Prasutagus is respectful and amiable. In others he is a spendthrift who is deeply in debt to the empire, giving them a hold over him and the right to seize his kingdom upon his death. In one version of the story, I read him as a fool. In another, he matches Boudica's intelligence and strength. Either version is a portrait in broad strokes that leaves most of the canvas blank. How did he die? Was he tall or short? Charismatic? Caring? Loutish? Funny? Did they share an equitable marriage, or was it troubled? Was he an absent father or an involved one? Did he rule fairly? Did he own pets? Ride horses? Hunt? What was his favorite food? Favorite memory? Favorite hobby?

And then there was the matter of the names themselves. Boudica and Prasutagus didn't exactly trip off the tongue. Film audiences have become accustomed to Roman names, but the Celtic ones added a new level of strangeness. The sounds of "Boudica" made me think of a lowing cow rather than a beautiful, strong, or intelligent woman. I could see why Sid Meier had gone with the Romanized version, Boadicea, but I wanted to honor the Celt she was.

Finally, there was the question of money, a question I preferred to ignore but that tickled in the back of my brain. My sister is a filmmaker, and I know from watching her career that financing even a small, low-budget film is a challenge. I had planned an epic, a potentially multimillion-dollar project that would require armies and horses and specialized settings. I was—I am—a nobody, but what I imagined was not a nobody's film.

In spite of these qualms, I plunged into the project. As I read about the Iceni Celts, I was struck by how forward-looking they were. Both women and men wore pants. They worked together, building round houses with thatched roofs and weaving plaid wool like proto-grunge badasses. Historic Britons may not have had written language (the Romans had them there), but they had discovered iron and produced intricate art. Celtic women fought alongside men and held leadership positions. The Romans used these facts to stress the barbarity of those whom they conquered, citing women warriors as evidence of a lack of civility, but from my twenty-first-century vantage point, the Celts' gender parity seemed eons ahead of chivalrous but patriarchal Rome.

The more I read, the more convinced I was of my screenplay's potential. Even the history seemed to have three acts, and the Roman texts were oddly cinematic. Centuries before cameras or human flight, Tacitus begins his section on Boudica with a helicopter shot, zooming us in:

> On the shore stood the opposing army with its dense array of armed warriors, while between the ranks dashed women, in black attire like the Furies, with hair disheveled, waving brands. All around, the Druids, lifting up their hands to heaven, and pouring forth dreadful imprecations, scared our soldiers by the unfamiliar sight, so that, as if their limbs were paralyzed, they stood motionless, and exposed to wounds. Then urged by their general's appeals and mutual encouragements not to quail before a troop of frenzied women, they bore the standards onwards, smote down all resistance, and wrapped the foe in the flames of his own brands.

The words sail us over the landscape and into the scene just as Randall Wallace's would bring us in over the Scottish Highlands to meet Mel Gibson. Not only that, but Tacitus even wrote a rallying speech in which Boudica urged her people to fight: "It is not as a woman descended from noble ancestry, but as one of the people that I am avenging lost freedom, my scourged body, the outraged chastity of my daughters." It might not have the same ring as Wallace's "They might take our lives, but they will never take our FREEDOM!" but it was something I could work with. Cassius Dio said that Boudica was tall and that a "great mass of the tawniest hair fell to her hips." He described her dressed in a tunic of diverse colors "over which a thick mantle was fastened with a brooch." I saw Cate Blanchett in the role: beautiful, deep-voiced, unflappable, intelligent, commanding. Boudica would have wit, I thought, but not a raucous one. I imagined a character that would push back against the Roman label "barbarian."

Boudica was the movie I had waited all my life to see. She was a feminist icon centuries before a feminist movement existed, and her story deserved to be told.

In his classic text *The Art of Dramatic Writing*, Lajos Egri insists that plays (and by extension, screenplays) must have a premise—a message, a point, a reason for the story to exist. As a fiction writer first, this felt overly simplistic to me. I believed Flannery O'Connor's stricture that a story "isn't really any good unless it successfully resists paraphrase, unless it hangs on and expands in the mind." Egri's "premise" sounded too much like the moral at the end of one of Aesop's fables, the lesson spelled out, reduced to a sentence, the bow neatly tied. Even so, I conceded that a story, whether written in prose or as a screenplay, should have a core question at its heart if it is to be relevant, and I gave this matter some thought.

As a reader and writer, I understood that historical fiction was as much about the culture and biases of the time of its writing as it was about the time in which it was set. Boudica lived in the Iron Age, but I inhabited the twenty-first century. In the early 2000s, I was interested in the violence of her story and how a colonized woman fought to retake her homeland. Shaped by the trauma of 9/11, I leaned into the problems I saw around me: how vengeance could skew sanity, how nationalism superseded the desire for peace, how violence spurred violence.

I imagined scenes that reflected these concepts, pitting the Romans and the Iceni in a game of brutal one-upmanship that neither could ever really claim to have won. I envisioned murdered Roman children hanging from trees like limp fruit. I saw Celtic villages razed, scattered with the blackened bodies of the innocent. How callous would a people have to be to look on such scenes and feel triumph? What would push them to the point where they forgot their own humanity? And, more important, what would allow them to come back to some degree of sense? What would it take to allow them to accept the losses and walk away, rather than instilling more pain on their enemy?

The questions fascinated and fueled me. For more than a decade I gathered material, squirreling away information and ideas while I worked on other projects. I debuted my first novel and drafted a second as well as publishing dozens of stories, poems, and essays while Boudica loitered in the back of my mind. I read books on screenwriting, getting a sense of its rigid formal constraints (not so different from some poetry) as well as the basics of formatting. I got a copy of Final Draft, and when I was awarded my first sabbatical in the fall of 2016, I decided the time had come to stop gathering and start writing the thing I would never be able to sell.

What I didn't expect was that the world would tip beneath my desk as I wrote, or that the rules for politics would change, or that I would wake up on the morning of Wednesday, November 9, 2016, to the knowledge that my country hated women.

I had known that too many people in power turned a blind eye to sexual and racial assault, but I didn't know that I lived in a country that would condone assault once it had been made public, let alone reward its perpetrator with our highest office. I could not fathom the depth of so many Americans' hatred for people of color. In the immediate aftermath of the election, I listened to stories of church bombings and Islamophobia and I listened to the president-elect's silence about those terroristic attacks. I listened as he instead ranted incoherent diatribes demonizing Latinx immigrants. Until that election, I had not realized that my country was a festering wound or that we would spend the coming years wading through its pus.

That is to say, I awoke that morning in an entirely different historical moment than I had inhabited the day before. Drowning in the depth of my own naïveté, I turned to my project and saw it through a new lens. I knew from my reading that Boudica wasn't the only Celtic woman leading her tribe. Cartimandua led the Brigantes in the north of what is now England. Others were unnamed or unrecorded, mentioned in Roman histories only as evidence of the Britons' backwardness. The fact hit me with new force: Celtic people had always been equitable when it came to gender and war. Women not only fought and died; they led. I noticed stories on the periphery as well—Germanic women fighting alongside men. I read with renewed awareness the stories of Asian and Middle Eastern women buried with weapons, suggesting that fighting was part of their identity. The Romans called this barbarism, but I could not agree. We had an oaf in the Oval Office wearing suits and long ties, the attire of a civilized man, but attire that went no deeper than the skin. Barbarism and civility had been badly, wrongly defined.

Before, I had pictured the Roman conquerors exactly as history and popular culture had given them to me: rational, well-meaning men who bequeathed us the very idea of democracy. In my mind, they spoke in the British accents of those early full-color epics. Now, democracy itself seemed to be a long con.

Of course I knew victors write history, but I hadn't read *enough* slant. Boudica's ire was driven by machismo and toxic masculinity. The same forces that stretched their roots through the history of the Roman Empire now bloomed in our own democracy. Our president-elect channeled Hollywood's mafia man, that modern Roman. He shaped himself as godfather to the country, demanding loyalty and favor for favor, and I began to wonder if, at the same time Rome spread a more people-centered form of government, it simultaneously spread a sexist culture that would limit the role of women in "civilized" countries for centuries to come.

Rome's underestimation of both Boudica's intellect and fight—their underestimation of a woman's abilities—was their downfall. Or their temporary downfall. What worried me was this: In the end, the sexist, limited thinking won.

"Defeat isn't a problem so long as the writer lays in an alternate victory to be read in its ashes," I wrote earlier, but I could see no alternate victory. Rather, Boudica's story was a tragedy that would continue to manifest again and again through history.

I wrote, then rewrote, a third act that refused to work. Boudica got sick or took poison, the histories said, but which? Of all the things for history to be fuzzy about, this was a big one. Central characters are supposed to take agency over their lives, to *act*. As I faced the options laid out by my Roman historians, I felt my choice to be clear: Boudica poisoned herself. In her final moment, she had agency and control.

Yet in every version I wrote, the scene refused to make sense. Self-poisoning in the face of defeat was a common trope of Roman stories, but though they read the act as noble, it seemed incompatible with what I knew. No matter how I imagined her character, no matter how cornered, I couldn't see a motivation for her to drink the vial. The odds were *always* stacked against the Iceni. The loss of one battle wouldn't make her so desperate. Boudica had been assaulted and seen her daughters raped, but she came away from the experience like a wrathful god, wreaking destruction on the Roman armies. What could Rome do to her that had not already been done? What changed?

And that's where I left the draft. The year ended, and with it my sabbatical. I laid the screenplay aside to focus again on my essays and novel. We could almost say this was the end, a tragedy, if not for the fact that Boudica lives with me. I've continued to reimagine the screenplay. I'm still working.

In the intervening years, the problems of the ending have returned me to the story's beginning. In the draft I wrote in 2016, in the absence of information, I wrote the death of Boudica's husband as a murder that emptied a throne so that Rome could take the land. The motivation for this action wasn't totally clear. As I had written things, Seutonius's absence had created a power vacuum in which a murder could transpire, but in the decades of Roman occupation, surely there had been other opportunities. Why murder Prasutagus now?

In 2018 I returned to the possibility that I had rejected: sickness. If Boudica had a communicable disease, she would have caught it from someone. Prasutagus, most likely. It would explain his death. Centuries before antibiotics, the Celts' only option would have been to turn to the Druids for help, and they would have no real cures to give. I saw Boudica leading an army through the English drizzle, unsleeping, plagued by the nightmare of her daughters' rape, the illness taking hold. The physical and emotional stress must have been enormous—more than a body could bear.

I realized that I had been wrong in thinking that Boudica's agency lay in taking poison. The story of Boudica was a story of ferocity and mental toughness, but at the end of the day, the fiercest fighter, male or female, inhabits a fragile human body. Boudica's agency lay in confronting Rome. Her defeat need not come at their hands or hers but from a microscopic pathogen transmitted by her husband. By 2020 and the start of the pandemic, I felt certain of this possibility. Love and infection were bound together, and each could corrupt the strongest person. The seeds of the ending lay, as always, in the opening scenes.

As a student, I was often frustrated with history textbooks. They felt disconnected from me, centered as they were on men's stories. Beyond that, I struggled with the approach to narrative itself. The first paragraph of a chapter would paint a vivid scene, but before we could inhabit it, the focus would change. We would telescope backwards to the big picture. We would get the numbers of the dead, the maps of battlegrounds, the end results, and my eyes would glaze over. I was interested in the smaller, human picture.

The value of creative writing, even when writing work that no one might see, is that if I approach it honestly and curiously, it allows me to live one person's history. To be my characters, even temporarily, I have to ask questions, to notice when the logic and motivation don't add up, to see the parts of personality that remain true and unalterable by time or culture or circumstance. I knew so much more than I had when I started—about screenwriting, about Rome, about fragility and strength, about democracy and sexism, about what it is that makes a person into a warrior. I began to think that perhaps the most important gender battle in history happened in AD 61 and was decided, not by a contest of strength or intelligence, but by the pure dumb luck of the wrong person catching a cold.

The question haunts me: What if Boudica had won? I think about the ripple effect of one moment in time. When I mention my project, most people have never heard of the Celtic warrior queen. Her story was nearly buried by time and by historians who couldn't see its value. It's still slipping away. In spite of statues and paintings and Sid Meier's *Civ II*, I fear she's becoming largely lost to us.

Boudica is a story about bodies: male and female, sick and well, colonized and colonizing. It's a story about power and possession. I need to jump back to the thing I haven't really discussed. It, too, is at the beginning, and it, too, may lead me to the end.

During my sabbatical, struggling with a fizzling third act, I emailed a draft of the screenplay to my sister. I knew I could trust her to be honest and bring the flaws to light. She would see the problem ending, but she might also be able to follow its roots back, finding the place in the story where I had first gone wrong.

Megan was enthusiastic, especially about a few of the side characters that I had invented and the love story I laid into their subplot. I had mostly gotten the formatting correct (thank you, handbooks) and she didn't raise any major questions about the structure, though she agreed that the ending wasn't as epic as it needed to be. Perhaps more important, she raised a question that I was blind to: how to handle the rape scene.

How many had I seen in my life? I couldn't number them. Rape, murder, and other violence against women so often spurred a film's action. Rape scenes had become a cliché of inciting incidents, sexual assault compelling male saviors to action. Perhaps only seduction scenes rely more heavily on the male gaze. Even the most sensitive rape scenes don't capture the horror of the experience. Instead, too often, they offer a perverse sympathetic pleasure for male viewers inclined to align themselves with the rapist rather than the victim.

When the election results had come in and history changed, my depiction of sexual assault, inspired by model films drawn from the past, had not. If my movie was to be a story of female power, I needed a new way to show rape.

The camera keeps viewers necessarily externalized. It objectifies the woman, just as her attacker does. Shown from this perspective, the rape scene, and thus the movie itself, participates in violence against women.

Laura Hudson's article for *Wired* magazine, "Rape Scenes Aren't Just Awful. They're Lazy Writing," concludes with a definitive tip: "Do not write a rape scene. While there are exceptions to this, everybody tends to think they are one of those exceptions, when more likely they are the reason the advice exists."

I felt the wisdom of this counsel, but also resisted it, wanting, like everybody, to see my screenplay as an exception. More than that, though, cutting the scene seemed akin to denying the existence of the story's crux. I didn't want to rewrite history. I didn't want to silence the generating moment of a story that had already been too silenced. Rape was essential to the sex, gender, and power issues running throughout Boudica's story. Formative. The outrage committed warps every character, male and female, bending them toward new and unimagined violence. In that initial act of hatred against women, we see the social attitudes that will ultimately prevail, that still prevail.

In the United States, our best estimates show one in six women is raped, though barely over a third of rapes are reported. In spite of #MeToo, it remains a largely hidden epidemic. As our country confronts and too often dismisses or excuses its now former president's assaults, I am recommitted to writing a story that probes the silence. Rape isn't one moment in time but a successive line of violences. Rape is a living brutality that persists both within the woman who survives it and within the society that permits rape to occur. My characters were not unscathed. Rather, their trauma erupts from the heart like Ridley Scott's alien, uncontainable and bleeding acid.

To leave the scene as written would be to make the audience voyeurs to sexual violence. To move it offscreen would be to erase the horror that sparked a war. One would make me a traitor to my sex, the other a traitor to her story. The scene requires a reimagination of how to write the camera's gaze, how to take the objective view and rob it of its default maleness, and I continue to mull possibilities, even as news of other high-profile rapes has rolled in: Christine Blasey Ford telling her history with Brett Kavanaugh, Chanel Miller confronting Brock Turner. I watch the women ridiculed; I see the men exonerated. And, powerfully, steadily, I watch women stand, speak their stories, fight. This is the story we have yet to see celebrated on-screen and the perspective I most forcefully need to inhabit: the assaulted woman who makes of herself a warrior.

In AD 60 or 61, a Celtic woman led the largest and most successful revolt ever launched against the Roman Empire on British soil. She fought until her body failed. However, when one body dies, the ideas and ideals it stood for do not die with it. By telling the story, we allow the dead to rise. Today I watch as the United States vacillates between calling out reprehensible behavior and apologizing for it. In the face of this aggression, women could give up, but we won't. We can't. That's not what warrior queens do. Rather, we take up the battle. Thinking of those who came before us, we hoist their flag with our own living arms and carry the fight forward, knowing the history and the odds, toward the possible but yet unrealized victory.

Idaho, 1994

In Idaho, in 1994, you believed you had never met a gay person. You were in college then, and you wondered how you would act when you finally did, whether you would be weird about it. You hoped not, but in Idaho, in 1994, homosexuality seemed, to you, a foreign thing. You embraced acceptance abstractly, an easy belief that had not been fully tested.

In your Contemporary Literature class, you sat in the middle of the room. To your right were farm kids, recognizable by their quilted flannels and worn Wranglers. You watched for the cute guy wearing a sweat-blackened, scab-colored Redskins cap that testified to years of unwavering fandom to a team you loathed. You disregarded his poor team choice and saw the cap instead as a hopeful sign of more general fidelity. Its brim broke through a frayed woolen edge, revealing the white plastic form that gave it shape.

To your left were lady stoners. Their thrift store clothing and broken-down boots spoke of another place entirely, one that salvaged Idaho's textiles and reinvented them into something wild. You'd stare at the green moon tattooed on the back of one girl's neck. You envied her overalls and the bravery it took to wear her hair unwashed, pillow-coifed. You envied, too, the tall girl you often saw rolling and smoking cigarettes on the steps of Brink Hall, listening to the old professor playing bagpipes on his lunch break. They were cooler than you, that much was certain. They walked into the classroom like it was the cheapest dive bar in the state. No one there could say a word to them.

Except that wasn't true. Not in Idaho. Not in 1994. She came in to class one day, the tall girl who rolled her own. She was not crying but had cried, her eyes puffy and red. The moon-necked girl asked what was wrong. The tall girl said that another kid from Salmon, her hometown, had called her mother and told her that her daughter was gay. Her mother told the girl, her daughter, that she could not come home again. Not now. Not ever. It wasn't that her mother didn't love her, though that seemed an issue still up for debate, but that she was certain her daughter would be killed now that the truth was out. Her home could no longer be her home.

It was Idaho, 1994. Richard Nixon would die that semester, as would Kurt Cobain. You sat in between farm kids and stoners. You were neither. They had seemed so untouchable, the cool group of girls whom you now recognized as gay.

The Internet was being built, and though the lab computers did not yet connect to the World Wide Web, they could connect to each other and a campus server. For the first time in your life, you were responsible for reading discussion posts. On the class forum, one of the farm kids commented that there were more slang words for penis than vagina, and the tall girl countered with a list of vulgarity that was itself an education. You wished you were as bold. You wished they would allow you into a conversation, invite you to share a joint, but you'd always had that thing in you that people recognized as other. Not farm kid, not stoner.

That year, a guy you had known as first chair flute from your high school band would attempt suicide, unable to reconcile his Catholic faith with his love of men. *Tony?* you would ask, realizing that you had always known. In another year, the manager at the store where you worked would be arrested for assaulting an Asian man, a stranger on the street for no reason that he, your manager, would specify. Four years later, Matthew Shepard would die on a Wyoming fence.

There are days when 1994 in Idaho feels like forever ago. How could you have been so naïve, so oblivious? You've changed in the years since. Learned. Grown. You thought the world had too, but this is another thing you were wrong about. Now, twenty-some years later, that fabric has worn thin, and you see Idaho, 1994, peeking through its weft and warp. You see the old, hard, white hatred that you first became acquainted with then. It pushes through, giving this moment its shape.

Digging into *The Dirt*

The Sexual Politics of Netflix's Mötley Crüe Biopic

I'd be lying if I said I hadn't always been conflicted about Mötley Crüe. On the one hand, they rocked. Play a Crüe song at a party and the party came to life. They pushed back against Reagan-era conservatism and the rise of the morality-bound Christian right with tunes that promoted sex positivity and good times. On the other hand, they were wantonly destructive— to hotel rooms, to women, to themselves. "Girls, Girls, Girls," they sang, chanting the old siren call from every roadside strip club. I hadn't read their book—had not, in fact, even known there was a book to read—but in the late eighties and early nineties I was as steeped in MTV culture as any good Xer. Debauchery was the Crüe's brand, and even then I knew that the freedom they embodied might as well have been labeled "men only."

This is to say, I thought I knew what I was getting into when I decided to watch Netflix's biopic *The Dirt*. One friend of mine had tweeted about how fun it was, how well it captured the spirit of the hair metal eighties. Another friend had watched it three times already. Mötley Crüe was *her band*, she'd told me. The movie brought back the thrill of her exuberant youth. *The Dirt* promised a joyful if mindless way to wind down after a long day, an escape from the constant stress of climate change, nuclear threats, trade wars, triggering tweets—not to mention work and family.

Knowing the band's history, I was only mildly surprised when the film's opening party showed Tommy Lee parting a girl's legs to perform oral sex, Nikki Sixx lighting the sleeve of his leather jacket on fire, and Vince Neil bending a nameless girl over the bathroom counter as he stares at himself in a concert poster. "He's not thinking about her," the movie tells us, as if we hadn't noticed that her only purpose is to be a bouncing set of boobs that underscore Neil's sexuality. Even so, I sat up when the film snapped me back to Tommy, now jumping away and calling to the crowded room, "Holy shit, guys, here it comes!" as the girl squirts either cum or urine across the room. I would later read that this was the scene the band was most looking forward to seeing when the film was released, though even they couldn't agree on what fluid was supposed to be spouting from the woman's vagina, a debate they aired publicly in Kory Grow's *Rolling Stone* article teasing the premiere.

The moment caps off a rough first two minutes, and it sets the film's trajectory. It alerts us to its stance on women and its troubled, perhaps Trumpian relationship with fact. Borrowed from pornography, the scene is fantasy rather than documentary, a romanticized version of one of the many parties that the band members will repeatedly tell us they can't remember.

From there, they only double down on their misogyny. The film jumps back in time to Sixx's abusive childhood and the mother who fails and fails him. We see the band's origin, and how they are nearly derailed by Vince Neil's girlfriend. ("Muzzle that," Nikki says.) We see Tommy, the self-proclaimed romantic, propose to a girl who will hit him, stab him with a pen, and repeatedly call his mother a cunt until Tommy lashes out and punches her—another woman overcome. Heather Locklear appears and vanishes, not important enough to be granted characterization. Sixx's mother reappears and is cast aside, another obstacle cleared. Even his drug addiction, which prevents Sixx from reaching out to Neil after his car wreck, is cast as female: "I'd fallen head over heels in love. And she was the sweetest thing I'd ever known. She made me feel all the warmth and happiness I never knew as a child. Her name was heroin." The message is clear: Women exist to give pleasure or to cause problems. In either case, Mötley Crüe's response is the same: Fuck 'em.

Every feminist bone of my body should have been triggered, and yet, my friends were right. The film was fun. The sarcastic and sardonic Mick Mars provides a necessary balance to the band's immaturity. He offers the sole defense of women, saying, "I happen to have respect for myself and for the females of the species," though this respect itself is never shown, since Mars is notably abstinent through the film. Lee bounces through scenes with warm sincerity. We're there when they name the group. We're there for the first show. We're on tour with Mötley Crüe—a privileged position. The film throws an arm around us and pulls us along. How can we judge a group whose members have so generously allowed us in? With them, we get to meet Ozzy Osbourne, witnessing as he snorts ants, pees poolside, and then laps up his own urine. The scene is appallingly absurd and should read as a tragic cautionary tale of what can happen to a man encouraged toward the worst excesses of drugs and alcohol, but the film asks us to see Ozzy as the band does: a mystical figure who lives a life beyond what mere humans can achieve. "I gotta hand it to you, Oz," Sixx says. "All these years and you're still keeping up with us kids." Ozzy replies, "Keeping up with them? I fucking lapped you, mate!" Around them, the squarest of 1980s yuppies reel back, appalled, and Doc McGhee laments, "I have managed the Scorpions, Bon Jovi, Skid Row, KISS. I have been dragged through the deepest shit with all kinds of mentally ill people. But I have never been through what Mötley Crüe put me through." If the point of the film is fun, then we're not to worry about lame morality or ethics. We are on the other side, Mötley Crüe's side.

Sure, *The Dirt* dips into darker moments: Sixx's descent into heroin addiction and his legendary escape from death, and (a tempered version of) the accident in which Neil's drunk driving costs the life of Hanoi Rock's front man Razzle.[1] Late in the film, Neil rejects the band's hard-won sobriety in favor of the alcohol and drugs that will get them through the tour, and the moment has a kind of inevitability. The tour has worn on them, and they dive back into a (perhaps?) modified version of their old addictive behaviors. Drugs and women provide the reprieve that turns to triumph: the tour is saved, the party goes on.

Maybe it was fine, I thought as the credits began. It was, after all, just a bit of fun.

Following the biopic cliché, the filmmakers included clips from the film alongside original footage of the band itself, but in this case the clips highlighted the differences rather than the similarities. The actors look

---

1 Grunge's "Lies The Motley Crue Movie Told You," www.youtube.com/watch?v=UuHvN 4l6amY, compares the facts to the film version of the accident; see minute 6:07–7:06.

innocent compared to the men they depict. In the film, Lee reads as boyish and goofy, Mars aloof, Neil befuddled, and Sixx stoically brave in the face of abuse. Yet when the images of the real men roll, they appear distinctly hardened.

The sequence threw me back, questioning what I had just watched. Mars is played by Iwan Rheon, familiar to audiences as Ramsey Bolton, the convincing sadist from *Game of Thrones*, but here he carries none of that threat. The film's Tommy Lee is so far from the real man that I didn't at first realize that he was supposed to be *the* Tommy Lee, thinking that he was a first, false-start drummer who would be replaced. Aside from the single punch, the film doesn't mention Lee's other charges of abuse, against either Pamela Anderson or his son. The actors play their roles brilliantly, but the casting softens our understanding of the action and makes men harmless who were not harmless.

The film's greatest source of joy is the music itself. *The Dirt* reminded me why I had always loved it—and how. I loved those songs like so many of my friends loved their cigarettes, knowing they were destructive but consuming them anyway. Singing "Dr. Feelgood" to myself after the credits played, I was literally moved. I danced. I willed myself to overlook the band's failings for the same reason I always had—if the music was good, maybe it didn't matter who made it. Besides, Mötley Crüe were old men, as obsolete and irrelevant now as the women they'd used and thrown aside. Surely I could continue to give them a pass.

Yet I spent the night unable to sleep. My mind returned again and again to the movie, refusing to let it lie. I couldn't stop thinking about it. I kept hearing the subtext it whispered: *Look at how much fun life was before we had to care that women had feelings.*

When I said this to friends, their response was almost uniform: Did you expect any different from Mötley Crüe? And no, I didn't—but I'm not talking about the band. I'm talking about the film, the creative text made in *this* moment. The credits list scores of people who collaborated, men and women, all of whom must have given at least a passing thought to the questions "Why this film? Why now?" IMDb lists seven writers: the four band members and the ghostwriter who worked with them on the book, along with two screenwriters. Netflix executives greenlit the film. People came together to compose shots, to edit them into a cohesive narrative, to cast the parts, to play the parts, to market the film.

I found myself again considering Trump's haunting, infamous comment that it's OK to grab women "by the pussy" because "they let you do it." Like the president, the members of Mötley Crüe are unlikely to ever be held accountable for their assaults. For one thing, where would we even start? Perhaps more important, though, their acts were never a secret. They bragged about them, and when we did nothing in response, or, worse, when we revered them as celebrities, it was as if the country had given its consent.

Recently, *Vice* uploaded a video titled "Conservatives and Progressives Debate Feminism, #MeToo, and Donald Trump," in which an interviewer talks to a group of women about why they cast the presidential votes they cast. One young African American defends her vote for Trump even in the light of that comment. "Trump said *groupies* will literally let you. Have you all never been around groupies? 'Cause they do. He just told the truth."

I want to judge her, I want to see her as a stupid Trump voter who is complicit in his dehumanization of women, but her wording grants agency to the women Trump referenced that few people of either party have granted. She sees the so-called groupies as autonomous beings, people with the choice to accept or reject his sexual advances. Her comments raise an interesting question of consent, yet her views still strike me as under-complicated. They are founded on the ideas that (1) groupies are a subset of women whom we can discount, and therefore assault is not a problem if it is perpetrated against them, a vicious kind of othering, and (2) celebrity power and the abuse of that power should not be weighed into questions of consent.

I can't agree to either premise. Unfortunately, *The Dirt* goes further, failing to grant to any women, let alone groupies, the humanity that is necessary for agency. As we're told, "Bottom line is, don't leave your girlfriend alone with Mötley Crüe. Ever! Because they'll fuck her!" The women in the movie can't make decisions. Only men have the decisive ability to leave their women with lascivious men or to take them away.

Netflix's biopic, however light and entertaining, participates in our national dialogue, and its message is far too familiar to women. We hear the same vapid complaint in news commentary, on social media, from stand-up comics, in hallway conversations. Women, we're told, have gone too far in asking for fair treatment. We've gone too far in suggesting that we be allowed to make decisions about our sexual encounters. We've gone too far in asking for protection from casual assault. We've spoiled the fun that "everyone" was having.

In her *Paris Review* piece "Nostalgia for a Less Innocent Time," Elisa Gabbert writes, "People think of nostalgia as a yearning for 'a more innocent time.' But I'm nostalgic for a *less* innocent time, or maybe for the way it felt to watch these scenes of decadence from the perspective of childhood innocence." I feel this so deeply. I've seen too much to watch Mötley Crüe from the innocent vantage I once had, and it's hard not to feel an element of mourning in that admission.

Like so many of my friends, I loved music that did not love me back. Sure, fun was the point, and God knows we could all use some fun right now, but I have come to accept that I need more than just a good time. Or, rather, I don't want to be corollary to fun, adjacent to fun, an object of fun. I don't want someone's fun performed on me or at my expense. It turns out, the specialists in fun were never really as good at it as they claimed. For all the appearance of innovation and novelty, Mötley Crüe and so many other bands practiced fun in old, narrow, unimaginative ways bound by gender and sexuality. Yet if we are willing, we can weed out those noxious, pernicious, and invasive ideals. In the dirt they plowed, we can cultivate a better, bigger, more welcoming party.

A Well-Turned Ankle

I am walking to the exit of the local dinosaur park, passing the plaster triceratops slide to a heavy metal gate worthy of Jurassic Park, when pain slides like a knife through the front of my ankle. I gasp, jump off my foot, but now it seems fine. I take three pain-free steps when the pain slides in again, then vanishes a step, then returns. My husband is far ahead of me now, talking with his sister, who's here for a visit. Our three nephews whirl like nectar-filled bees around my son and brother-in-law. Only my fifteen-year-old daughter is near enough to see me suddenly, sporadically gasping and limping. "Are you OK?" she asks. I tell her what's happening. The distance between us and the rest of the family grows as the boys race to cars for the ice cream we've promised. "Do you need me to have Dad pull the car up?" my daughter asks. The car is across the road, maybe fifty yards away. I am tougher than this—an almost athlete, a wannabe badass—but "Yes," I say, incredulous that I can't make so short a distance, though now even lifting my foot even half an inch to clear the grass sends a fresh knife sliding in. I have no idea how I'll heft it up into the passenger foot well of our car. My toes somehow now weigh fifty pounds apiece, each fully capable of sending a blade again and again through the front of my ankle.

This is an essay about chasing perfection:
The day before the knife started its slide, I had run up and down and up and down the stairs of our split-level home, setting up the guest room for the boys and finding books and toys and games they might like and pulling a *Star Wars* tiki mug out of storage for the oldest and then running down to find another for the middle child and then another for the youngest. I became something frippery and fluttering, making cocktails and finding

special plates and doing everything I could to be the perfect aunt and hostess, the perfect mother, the perfect wife. I was, I am, determined to show my husband's family how well he's chosen in picking me for his life partner. I do this every time his family visits, and though I always chastise myself afterwards for turning into a pie-baking 1950s pastiche of femininity, this is the first time my body itself has actively revolted.

This is an essay about self-sabotage:
I don't visit the doctor until they leave. In intervening days, the pain has vanished for an hour here, twenty minutes there, only to continually return, bringing tears to my eyes. I've iced; I've Adviled; I've elevated my ankle on cushions. These things work only as long as I make myself sit, but as the pain recedes, I find myself up again, wiping up a spill, fixing a snack, smiling and chattering until their minivan pulls out of the driveway en route to the next stop of their driving vacation. No one is asking me to do this.

This is an essay about the problems of a failing, aging body:
The doctor palpates my ankles, each in turn. "The tendons are swollen," he tells me. He asks if I do any sports. "Running, tennis, and horseback riding," I answer. He shakes his head and laughs. "Yeah, this is an overuse injury," he tells me. He tells me to lay off everything for a couple weeks and return slowly.

I broke myself walking in a park or I broke myself running up and down a single flight of stairs. Either way I see this, it seems impossibly stupid. I have never seen myself as fragile. "He diagnosed me as being in my forties," I once heard a friend say after his doctor visit. I suspect I've just been handed the same diagnosis.

This is an essay about curiosity:
I search the Internet for more information, wanting to know what is going on under my skin. Anterior ankle tendon injuries are, apparently, rare. That's what site after site tells me. From what I understand, when the anterior tendon swells to a certain point, it rubs on the bone. This is the source of pain; I am the knife as well as the body it stabs.

This is an essay about denial, an essay about body image, an essay about fear:

I lay off everything but walking. Our puppy is six months old and needs exercise and training and I'm the one who insists on leash manners. Also, if I don't move my body, I will gain back all the weight I carried in high school and college. If I gain back the weight, I will become angry at my image in the mirror and in photographs. Fat will build up in my brain, and I will have a stroke like my mother and lose my mind to vascular dementia. These fears are not entirely rational, but that does not matter. I buy ankle braces and high-top tennis shoes, anything I can think of to offer support. I ice. The ankle is taking longer than it should take to heal, months rather than weeks. I return to the doctor for x-rays, but nothing is broken, so the prescription remains the same: rest.

This is an essay about dumb, everyday, unexciting injury:

I hobble around. I consider tying a string to my toes so that I can work my foot like a marionette.

This is an essay about the failings of the American medical system:

I return to tennis in late summer and light running in the fall, but in spite of the time they've had to heal, my ankles become swollen and achy after exercise. I make an appointment to see a sports medicine specialist. The receptionist tells me the doctor will want to take x-rays and I let her know that I already have had them. Because the doctors are in different networks, I have to make a special trip, but I collect the images on CD from my general practitioner and take them with me to my appointment. The receptionist tells me again that the sport medicine doctor will want x-rays, and when I say again that I have them, she says he'll want better ones, though how this can be determined without even touching the disc is a mystery. I repeat the same conversation with the nurse who takes my weight and history. When the doctor enters, he comes in saying, "Yes, we'll need new x-rays." He has not yet said hello to me or glanced at my face or my foot. He has not asked, "What seems to be the problem?" When I repeat, yet again, that I've had x-rays, he scrolls through the images on the computer, barely glancing at them before telling me that they're not good enough, that none of them are "weight bearing," though I am looking at an image of my bones on his screen, and my foot is clearly bearing weight.

This is an essay about the desire to please male authorities:
I feel the doctor's anger when I decline. I have irritated him, and all I have to do to make him happy is shoot radiation into my bones. The tactic is not ineffective: I want to make him pleased with me. He tells me that insurance will cover most of it and I probably won't have to pay more than $75. He says this as if $75 were nothing and is surprised when, again, I refuse. I know, even as I do, that my problem is mostly one of tone: if he had talked to me first and looked at the x-rays and then asked for new ones, I would have complied. But this demand for x-rays feels too brazen. I feel like he doesn't give a damn about me, let alone my ankle. I feel like he's using me to supplement his season ski pass at Snow Basin. The doctor tells me to try new shoes and leaves me to find my own way out. I think of all the senators who insist that medical care is cheaper when patients take ownership of their care, but I'm out a $45 copay, supplemented with insurance, and I received no care. I didn't even receive a passable replica of care. If my pain were worse, if I were more desperate, how fast would I have paid this man for the x-rays he claims to need?

This is an essay about body image:
In the absence of professional care, I treat my own damned self. I read web articles and watch YouTube videos. I believe in strength training and physical therapy. I believe that if I can strengthen the muscles in my legs, I will have fewer problems with my ankles. Unfortunately, this means going to the gym. This means the hall of mirrors. It means spandex and white lights. It means men's eyes. I vow to go in spite of all these things. I block time on my calendar. I pack bags with shoes and clothes so that I can head to the gym directly from my office. I do everything I need to do, and yet I don't go.

This is an essay about a body part:
I ice my ankles. I keep them wrapped. I take double doses of pain killers. I stretch before and after exercise, the only thing that actually seems to help. I will power through and recover because this is what I do. I think of the

phrase "a well-turned ankle." I think of Victorians and fetishes, femininity and strength. I think about how the ability to walk upright is human, how on a horse or dog or cat, an ankle is a hock and a knee is a stifle, and how as a child I misunderstood animal knees as backwards. I think of how much is hidden in the interior landscapes of our bodies and how much can be read on those maps. I think about how one small, isolated story of a part can be the sum of so many wholes.

Nakedness

Full nakedness! All my joys are due to thee;
As souls unbodied, bodies unclothed must be,
To taste whole joys.
   —John Donne, "Elegy XX: To His Mistress Going to Bed"

1.

I used to scrub the bathtub naked. There wasn't anything alluring about this. Scrubbing naked was merely practical and efficient. I ruined fewer shirts with bleach stains if there was no shirt to ruin, and after scrubbing I could wash both the sweat from my body and the cleanser from the walls in one turn of the faucet.

I know it's supposed to be different. I've seen the ads. The women in those domestic spaces may be covered, but what nakedness we get suggests the perfection of the unseen body. I remember the woman fixing a kitchen sink, her Daisy Dukes pulled low by her tool belt, her flannel shirt knotted at the midriff to show off her flat, tanned belly and curving waist. The ad winks at us. Isn't it cute, this woman doing man's work in this safely domestic space? I imagine her husband cracking a PBR and watching the game. I can't now remember what she was selling, but I can see the image even now. Her work, her body, staged and lit and photographed, was a portrait of male desire.

My own working body? Not so much. Things jiggle that should not jiggle, and even the things that should jiggle increasingly jiggle more than is becoming. My belly, crosshatched with the stretch marks that chronicle two pregnancies, glows fish white because I am not in the habit of revealing it for public view. For me, nakedness has always felt not like exhibition or exhilaration but like exposure.

My body is a private and practical thing. I've yielded it to the production of children and the scrubbing of a bathtub. And yet, here I am, sitting in front of a computer, writing it into view, offering its naked portrait to the public because, as a writer, it is part of my job to be publicly naked.

I'm not the first writer to draw the comparison between writing and nakedness.[1] For manly poets (take Ginsberg and Whitman), the naked body is powerful. With phalluses dangling, they are free to sound barbaric yawps over the rooftops of the world, shouting their hopes for democracy and art and America. Their nakedness is bold, a nonverbal "fuck you" to the social convention of clothed bodies. They eat from the tree of knowledge, munching their apples with smacking gums and an utter lack of shame. Like a boy responding to a triple dog dare, the male poet summons his bravado and exposes himself to speak on behalf of all those clothed in our own silence.

Only male nakedness affords boldness and bravado. "Full nakedness!" John Donne exclaims ecstatically in "To His Mistress Going to Bed," but even there the naked female body is an object of pleasure, not a subject of strength. She is a land to be conquered ("O my America! My newfound land!") or a book to be uncovered ("mystic books, which only we / ... / Must see reveal'd"), but the only contents he's truly interested in are the contents of her girdle. Nakedness grants women temporary control over male attention, but it distracts from the quality of our ideas rather than punctuating them. To be naked is to draw attention away from the mind and onto the body. To be naked is to be vulnerable. Our bodies are soft. Desire hangs in the air around us, threatening to metastasize into rape.

Women don't fare much better in folklore. According to legend, her people, suffering under the weight of heavy taxes, turn to Lady Godiva to appeal to her husband, the Earl of Mercia. He responds with a dare: If she is willing to ride naked through the center of town, he will grant her

---

1   Kathleen Margaret Lant explores this very topic in her brilliant essay, "The Big Strip Tease: Female Bodies and Male Power in the Poetry of Sylvia Plath," revealing how deeply gendered our conceptions of nakedness are.

petition. In terms of the old sexist stereotypes, this seems like a way to shut her up, but Godiva unclothes herself and rides a white horse through the town's square, thus gaining the wish of the people and improving their well-being. While Lady Godiva appears to gain power through her unclothed body, it is a false power. Ultimately only her husband can lower the taxes. Godiva performs a social function only by allowing herself to be utterly exposed, sexualized, vulnerable.

The ride made her famous. Godiva has appeared in paintings and poetry and pop culture. Plath wrote, "Like white Godiva, I unpeel," and I've unpeeled the chocolate named for her. On television, Cersei Lannister's nude walk of shame invokes Godiva's legend. We might not remember the reason, but we remember the ride and, more important, we remember her nakedness. We remember the exposure.

Am I another Godiva when I tell you I scrub the bathtub naked? Is there a function to this exposure, or am I more like a flasher, opening my trench coat? "Sex sells," my students tell me in essay after essay. As a woman, I am not sure that I can write my body innocent of that old truism, yet I have put it on page after page.

2.

My daughter was born twelve days before the start of my PhD program. As a graduate teaching assistant, I had no maternity leave. I needed to earn my wages. Quietly and heavily bleeding into thick pads, I stood faint in front of my new students. I cut each hour-long class short on my first day back, dizzy and weak from the effort of simply standing and talking, but I had a job to do, and I completed the semester with no more shortened sessions and no missed classes, though the blood loss would continue for weeks.

Nothing has ever made me so aware of my own body as a practical thing as motherhood. My breasts wept milk as I plotted a novel. Friends of mine have written poetry about the beauty of breast-feeding, but I felt only like a cow to be milked. Hormones buzzed in my blood, chemically tweaking my already amped emotions. I found new depths to fear, terrified that if I showered while my child slept, I would return to find that she had died—from choking or from SIDS or from something I could have prevented if only I hadn't so selfishly washed myself. I nursed and I taught and I worked on the dissertation that many years and revisions later would become my first novel. Meanwhile my daughter lay in an electric swing or in a carrier by my foot or in the next room, not quite neglected, not quite mothered.

My guilt came to a head one everyday afternoon. As I worked, she cried the kind of cry that let me know she wanted me, but not the kind of cry that suggested an emergency. I tried to finish typing my thought, capturing it before it fled, my flustered fingers fumbling as I rushed so that I could run to comfort her. I held her for a while, loving her and allowing her to feel that love, but nonetheless aware of the siren call of the blinking cursor, the unwritten words that had to be written if I was ever going to finish school and earn something more than a graduate stipend. I put her in her play saucer and returned to my work, trying to find the words but again constantly aware of the child who needed me. Years before Ron Swanson would tell Leslie Knope not to half-ass two things but to whole-ass one thing, I faced that same certainty. I couldn't be both of the things I needed to be. Trying to do both, I was a shitty mother and a shitty writer in the same moment, and I was failing those I cared about, her most of all.

I had never been so aware of the pure egotism driving my desire to write as I was in that moment. As a mother, I wanted to put my child's needs before every other concern, but if I abandoned my book, I was giving up on the aspiration for which I had sacrificed so much. Between my teaching assistantship and my husband's paltry adjunct pay, we were as broke as we had ever been. Daycare was a luxury we couldn't afford. One of us taught while the other tried to watch the baby, clean the house, fix the meals, grade papers, and prepare our classes. Once a week, a fellow grad student would help watch her while I took class and he taught, but mostly we handed her off, often literally, driving her to campus so we could pass her like a living relay baton. Even so, the slender paychecks never stretched far enough.

How could I justify writing a novel—a pure flight of fancy—when doing so required the time and attention I might have reserved for my daughter? I asked myself the question daily, felt it voiced in the glances of colleagues, and heard it in phone calls from family members on the other side of the country. It didn't help that, like many writers, I often dreaded writing. Writing might be what I most wanted to do on the large scale, but on any given morning I could list a dozen things I'd rather do than face my own inadequate words, that ever-growing catalog of small failures. Add an infant who needed me into the mix, and writing felt impossible and selfish.

On that afternoon, as my now quiet daughter watched a battered VHS copy of *Baby Mozart*, I stared at the blinking cursor, trying in vain to think how the plot should unfold, unable to leave the world inhabited for the world I wanted to create. I told myself I could stand up, right then. I could shut the computer, walk away, never write again. I could live a perfectly happy and satisfying life. Maybe I'd return to teaching seventh-grade English, or maybe I'd grow organic vegetables in Oregon. Why not? Wasn't that what I was supposed to do?

I knew my Victorian literature and all its angels of the hearth. I'd read Sarah Stickney Ellis's *Women of England* and understood that, for centuries, we've believed that women serve their country's social good by raising children to understand both love and morality. Women's social function was served through their domestic work. Sure, we'd ostensibly moved on from all that those long-moldering Victorians believed, but I knew the basic presumption was still there: a good mother does *not* ignore her very real children to invent fictional characters.

And so I sat there wallowing in my maternal failure, my hands hovering over the keyboard and my eyes on my daughter. I realized I was thinking, even now, of myself, of what I was doing badly, and I shifted my focus. I started to think of her instead. If my only purpose was to be a mother, then what was I telling my daughter about her life's purpose? If I gave up on my writing, was I showing her that she must likewise become a mother, cede her own goals to the greater social good, and do nothing but raise morally sound children, whatever that meant? If she had daughters of her own, what purpose did their lives serve? Were we just mothers making more mothers making more mothers? Where did it end? Were we to be just one long chain of women sacrificing themselves on the altar of motherhood? Or could we want something more?

OK, I thought, so my writing was self-centered. Maybe that was the point. Maybe I loved my daughter best by *not* serving her every small desire, by showing her that it was fine to strive, that it was fine to work for an utterly selfish goal. Maybe by writing, I was modeling a new and powerful idea: The self is worth attending, no matter to what sex that self is attached.

I realized I wanted my child to see me in the act of writing, even if my novel never saw the light of day. My daughter and, eventually, my son should know that I will fail as often as I succeed. They should witness this firsthand. They should know that I could put it all aside and bake cookies and casseroles because cookies and casseroles are delicious and feed many people, but because they see me make the choice to write, they will know and I will know again that it is important that we each do the work we are compelled to do. They must know that, male or female, they have the same permission. This is a right.

3.

I'm left with the haunting image of Godiva. The problem is this: while writing for myself might give my children a distant sense of freedom to achieve their own desires, I'm still left with the image of scrubbing a bathtub naked—exposure, futility, and, most important, a need to achieve a larger end. I don't just want to write; I want to write for publication and, in my big dream moments, in moments when I allow myself the hope that our world will endure, for posterity. I write myself naked in front of the eyes of any reader/stranger who happens upon my work, now and for years to come. I want to be honest with myself: This is more than a feminist act on a small family scale. This is ego writ large.

Plato said that "poets are the unacknowledged statesmen of the world," and though I don't believe that either poetry or fiction that aspires to the quality of poetry must necessarily have a political agenda, Plato is right. Writing may be a solitary act, but writing for publication—writing for the public—makes the personal political and serves social change. It's not sexy. There are no low-slung Daisy Dukes and tanned midriffs, things jiggle that shouldn't jiggle, and sometimes we see the stretch marks, but poets and other writers, by exposing their deepest, most private, most individual and most vulnerable selves, ask us to understand the world in more intimate ways.

The mind of the writer, stripped naked and riding horseback down Main Street, enacts sacrifice and humility that contain no inherent power of their own, but call the larger world to act with purpose and responsibility. Perhaps the spectators will close their eyes and turn away, but some Peeping Tom or other will look and be affected by the looking. Such is the writer's contract with the community.

In recent decades, women poets have been claiming a powerful nakedness as mothers. In her poem "Bite Me," Beth Ann Fennelly gives a graphic account of the birth of her child, telling us that she pushed so hard she shat, that her asshole turned inside out, that the whites of her eyes were red with blood. The taboo experience of childbirth, so often covered over, clothed in stories of sweetness and light, is unflinchingly brutal. Fennelly exposes herself, yet rather than seeing nakedness as weakness, Fennelly claims for herself a traditional icon of male strength, the boxer, in triumphing through the utterly female act of birth. Her husband may be "terror and blood spatter," but she has fought the hard fight.

Reimagined—or, perhaps more accurately, stripped of imagined niceties—motherhood provides women with one of the few images of unclothed female strength. If you've been laid on a delivery table, your vagina out for all to see, battling through the tearing, gut-cramping agony that has become the metric by which other pain is measured—that is, if you have endured childbirth—you have a claim to strength. The first thing I learned in becoming a mother was how to be naked in front of others, spending years pulling my breasts from my shirt to feed children in spite of public staring and shaming. There are plenty of people still uncomfortable with women who expose their bodies, especially for practical purposes.

I'll admit, Godiva was the last thought on my mind as I put my own feet in the delivery bed's cold metal cups. Now I can't help but be struck by the metaphor I didn't know I was making. I had put my feet in the stirrups.

4.

When I was completing the final revisions of my novel before publication, when the reality that my words were about to be exposed to strangers came fully home, I had to remind myself again and again that writing at its best is more than just egomaniacal exhibitionism. I kept thinking of Anne Bradstreet, who in her poem "The Author to Her Book" famously addressed her creation as "Thou ill-formed offspring of my feeble brain." Mothering a book does not feel empowering. It feels nerve-wracking. As much as she tries to dress the book up, she says "nought save homespun cloth i' th' house I find," and she fears that her brain-child must walk "'mongst vulgars" in this feeble clothing. The book may not be naked, but all the clothes she can muster aren't enough to protect it.

I wanted to feel only the naked strength of motherhood, a la Beth Ann Fennelly, but I was consumed by the same fears and self-consciousness as Bradstreet. And yet ironically, rather than trying to trim the book in finer attire, I found myself trying to make it more naked. I went on daily "darling hunts," scrutinizing my manuscript for those moments of self-indulgence where I, the writer, wanted to show off, putting faith in language rather than story. "Murder your darlings"—the old advice. Let it bleed! Cut the flab! As if the book were in need of liposuction and a little nip/tuck.

Here's a thing I believe: If a novelist is writing well, she goes beyond nakedness and into transparency; she becomes as invisible to her audience as Wonder Woman's jet. Self-indulgent prose makes readers aware of the author, exposing the wrong body. Writing, if it is to become pure story, pure art, should instead expose the naked emotion while making the reader forget the writer altogether.

I'd really like to return to my first metaphor here and say that if the writer is naked enough, the reader sees only the gleaming bathtub and not the woman who made it so, but a tub seems too mundane. I need something grander, something less domestic. I'd like an image so free of connotation that it allows us to ignore bodies and gender and transcend to something sublime. All my metaphors are failing me. Ultimately, even in my best moments, I am still a body, a female body, tapping away at computer keys, sipping a coffee and needing to pee. Nothing I can think of lets me forget the basic, corporeal fact of myself.

5.

What's your *point*? I ask myself and ask myself, struggling to end this essay.

But having a point seems awfully phallic, and maybe that's not what I'm after here. Maybe all my questions are just a kind of scab I want to pick. Perhaps there is blood underneath, or perhaps something is healing. Any true metaphor seems connected to bodies. I've heard more than one person say that, in the modern era, we've become so detached from our physical experience that the purpose of the body is to transport the head. I don't believe that. I'm not sure thought outside of bodily experience is even possible.

I haven't scrubbed a bathtub naked in ten years or more. I couldn't tell you why I stopped, why even that private domestic moment began to feel too exposed. *Be naked*, I have charged myself, but the naked truth is that I am not sure I'm any closer to saying how I expect this nakedness to be empowering to anyone, myself included. *Que sais-je?* I wrote a book, I had it published, some people read it, and now I've written more.

I have birthed two children, one daughter and one son, and raised them while writing two novels, a short fiction chapbook, and this essay collection. Both of my children are smart and kind and independent. My son once complained that I hadn't been fun since I "started writing a book"— since before he was born, that is. I know the remark was born of jealousy for the hours I spend on my fiction. I know, too, that my attention and love are the water he swims in, so ubiquitous and expected that it's difficult to notice. I know how much fun I have had with him and my daughter, the twin lights that illuminate my life.

Even so, he isn't wrong. The hours I pour into a computer don't provide much entertainment, either for him or for me. I could have devoted that time to family. The hours were fruitless by many measures, because I'm not exactly writing best sellers and the chances of any of these words standing the test of time are so scant as to be nonexistent. I have one short life. What the fuck am I doing? The question is a familiar self-flagellation. I remind myself that I'm supposed to be past all this, that I made up my mind years ago, that it's for them. Even so, I feel the pulling opposition of the words "working mother."

Maybe this is what it looks like to tear at the social fabric, to strip oneself of the agreed-on roles. Maybe this is how we learn the precise shape of the naked, pointless, human mess underneath.

Acknowledgments

I am indebted to the editors at the journals that first published these essays
and gave them some love—

"Bread," *Oregon Literary Review*
"Building Tall," *Clackamas Literary Review*
"Cunt," *Indiana Review*
"Damage: The Soul-Crushing Science of High-End Bra Shopping,"
    The Rumpus
"Digging into *The Dirt*," *Change Seven*
"Dislocated," *Mary: A Journal of New Writing*
"Evening: Super Bowl XLVIII," *Hobart*
"The Gun That Won the West," *Prairie Schooner*
"I Am Woman," *March Badness*
"Idaho, 1994," *7×7 Special Issue: Legislating Bodies*
"My First Name," *Hobart*
"Nakedness," *So to Speak*
"The Only Girl in the Known Universe," *Change Seven*
"Taking It to the Logo," *Booth*
"A Well-Turned Ankle" (under the title "Ankle"), *Pithead Chapel*
"Wonder Woman," *Jellyfish Review*
"The World Within, the World Without: A Thought List," *Juked*
"Writing *Boudica*," *Miracle Monocle*

Extra special shout-out to Aaron Burch, whose comments on "My First
Name" made it a better essay.

I'm deeply grateful to the entire team at University of Georgia Press
as well as their extra-Press team members, including my wonderful copy

editor, Ann Marlowe, and the anonymous, generous reviewers who first gave this collection their support.

I would also like to thank my friends at *Barrelhouse*, both for making Writer Camp a thing and for always cheering me on and up, and my students and colleagues at Weber State University. Perhaps most important of all, I want to thank my graduate cohort at University of Georgia, in particular Melissa Crowe, Anastasia Lin, Valerie Morrison, Keely Byars-Nichols, Dan Shaw, Jamie McClung, and Carly Bonar, who watched my daughter, often for no other pay than my gratitude, so that I could complete my degree. They say it takes a village to raise a child, but sometimes a small group of caring friends is village enough.

Finally, massive and endless thanks to my family: Marie, Peter, and Megan Griffiths, and Nathanael, Gwendolyn, and Oliver Myers. You let me be me and love me anyway, and I love you right back.